CW00538770

Whispers of wisdom

Whispers of Wisdom

Reassurance for those living with loss

Tom Gordon

wild goose
publications

www.**ionabooks**.com

Contents

Dedication

To my parents, Jimmy and Jean Gordon,
who taught me much in life, and with whom
the continuing bonds of love remain ever strong.

Preface

Bereavement is integral to the human condition, and therefore none of us will be immune to the effects of grief and loss throughout our lifetime. For some, there will be too many bereavements to deal with, such that the cumulative effect over time becomes a heavy load to bear. For others, one specific death might have a devastating and crippling effect, causing an individual to doubt their capacity to cope and find a new and meaningful life beyond their loss. But, for everyone, bereavement takes us into an often unknown and uncharted world, which can be bewildering and scary, and which puts a strain on any inner resources we believed we had to cope with life's tragedies and traumas.

That means, therefore, that every single one of us in our grief and loss needs not only to find some way of making sense of what bereavement does to us, but to find someone, anyone, who can be our companion in this confusing new world, to wait with us with understanding, tolerance and empathy, till clarity emerges and we are able to take tentative steps towards a new beginning.

Where, then, are such people to be found? Where is this patient and sensitive support?

There are some who will say that we live in a more open and understanding society – that we know more about loss, can talk more openly than we once did, and that support is, therefore, more readily available and accessible. That may or may not be true. But it is my experience that whatever changes there have been in our society in recent generations, these have not translated into a more patient approach to dealing with bereaved people or the provision of more readily available support. On the contrary, in processing issues of loss and grief, I believe things have got worse rather than better for those who are bereaved.

We live in more isolated units than we have ever done. The

pressure society places on us to function, fulfil our role, get back to normal after a death is greater than it has ever been. Those who are bereaved are forced into patterns of behaviour and expected attitudes – in other words, to clearly exhibit coping strategies – before there has been any meaningful processing of their issues of grief. As a result, bereaved people find themselves pushed further and further into isolation and 'aloneness', with fewer opportunities than they need to check out or normalise their strange, new, scary and bewildering feelings.

This book – a follow-up to *New Journeys Now Begin* which was published in 2006 – is offered as an 'antidote' to the inability of our present societal structures to offer appropriate support to those who are bereaved. It is based on my engagement with bereavement issues throughout my working life – twenty years as a Church of Scotland parish minister, fifteen years as a hospice chaplain and co-facilitator of the hospice's bereavement support service, ten years of scoping, developing and facilitating the Acorns bereavement support programmes in Edinburgh and five years with the parallel Stepping Stones programmes in East Lothian. Alongside all of that, there has been my continued writing, training and teaching around issues of loss, grief and bereavement. If that knowledge and experience does anything, it illustrates the value of offering to bereaved people accessible support which is relevant, interactive, grounded and enabling.

But I'm seeking in this book to do even more than that. I want bereaved people to have a voice, to offer their tentative whispers or loud cries of anguish, to articulate their successes and failures, to share insights and to pose questions. I want them to have a place to say, 'This is me! And if I'm reacting normally to my bereavement, this might well be you too.'

If this book offers a glimpse of that, and as a result helps you, or those for whom you are concerned, feel less isolated and more understood in their grief, then it will have done its job. Gentle whispers of wisdom might fall on the ears of the people who need to hear them the most, help them feel and know that they, too, are normal, and above all reassure them that there *are* people out there who genuinely care and seek to understand.

This book – and any insights I have gained in bereavement issues – would not have been possible without the help, support and encouragement of many people.

The Acorns bereavement programmes are a product of the concern of William Purves, a long-standing family firm of funeral directors, for their client group and the wider community. The company continues to underpin Acorns financially and to offer support in many other ways. Thanks are due, therefore, to John Purves – now retired – for the original concept; James Morris, Chief Executive; Tim Purves, Board Chairman; and many others in the company for their unending interest in and support for what we do.

For the delivery of the Acorns programmes, we owe immense gratitude to Ailsa Hill and Helena Heveran, our team leaders; to the indispensable Hazel Strachan, whose contribution to every Acorns programme is immeasurable; to Susan Beatie, Marion Chatterley, Brian Embleton, Mairi Findlay and Donna Hastings for their work in our groups; to Kellie Anderson, Chris Jones, James McDonald and Dr Mike Wilson, our current resource people in their specialist fields, and others who have preceded them; and to countless other people who have contributed to the success and development of Acorns in large and small ways.

The Stepping Stones programmes are delivered through my own local church, Chalmers Memorial Church of Scotland in Port Seton, East Lothian, and are similar in style, content and approach to those of Acorns. The value of these programmes for the local community and for the wider East Lothian network is based on the concern of successive ministers and key office-bearers in Chalmers Church over many years. Tribute, therefore, should be paid to Rev Robin Alison and the Kirk Session of the church for their continued support and encouragement; to Joyce Buchanan, Ian Bulloch, Loreen Courtney, Elizabeth Glover, Mary Gordon, Amanda Johnston, Moyra Kaminski and Lyn Marshall for their sensitivity and insight in the delivery of the programmes; to Moira Copland, Phyllis Hogg, Dr Norman Wallace, Fiona Wardle and the staff and management of the Musselburgh Citizens' Advice Bureau for their input as resource people; to the staff and management committee of the Port Seton Community Centre for their unfailing support for the service we deliver.

I am immensely grateful to the family of the late Andrew Robertson for their gracious permission to tell the story of Andrew's death and the arrangements for his funeral service which I've included in Chapter 13. It is their hope and mine that through the pain and the sadness of this loss, another 'Whisper of Wisdom' might be heard that can be a help and encouragement to others.

Thanks are also due to Sandra Kramer, Publishing Manager at Wild Goose Publications, for her unfailing patience, diligence and good sense; to the many people, family, friends and strangers, who have encouraged me in my writing; to my wife Mary for her lasting support, wisdom and affirmation and with my grateful thanks for her cover photograph and for the designs of the images with which each chapter begins; and for all those, known and unknown, who have found my writing in various publications helpful and enlightening.

The most important and heartfelt thanks, however, must go to the countless number of bereaved people – named and unnamed – from whom I have learned over many years; for the trust they put in me and my colleagues, a trust which, I hope, has never been misplaced and which – and they're the only ones who'll really know what this means – has made a difference to their ability to cope with their bereavement and given them a glimpse of a workable and fulfilling future. They are the ones who have done the work, while we have only given them a framework in which that might be possible; they are the ones who have found resources in themselves to cope, while we have only offered indicators of where these resources might be; they are the ones who have grown in confidence, while we have been in awe of how their lives have changed before our very eyes; they are the ones who have offered whispers of wisdom, while we, myself included, have been privileged to listen, absorb their insights, and pass them on to others who might find them useful.

***

While the manuscript of this book was being edited, we were hit by the Covid-19 pandemic. As a consequence, an additional chapter has been included as a reflection on the effect a year of social restrictions may have on people's coping strategies in their bereavements. This most recent chapter also explores possible future complexities for individuals and communities as they seek to cope with deaths which have occurred during the pandemic.

In addition, the Acorns and Stepping Stones bereavement support work referenced here has had to be suspended, given that the work of both organisations is based on people being drawn together in small groups, where closeness and human contact is integral to what is being offered. It had been hoped that the suspension of this group-work would be temporary. However, the longer we've had to live with social restrictions, the harder it has been to redesign the work and to be clear about a realistic timescale. A decision has been made, therefore, to put a permanent hold on the work. It is hoped that, once restrictions have been lifted, an approach to bereavement work will evolve which will be appropriate to very changed circumstances. But what form that work will take is unfortunately, at the time of writing, far from clear.

Chapter 1

Is anybody listening?

I'm not particularly well informed about the structures and cultural norms of the indigenous societies of the North American continent. But on a recent visit to Canada I was fascinated by some of the legends and customs I heard about and the various artefacts associated with them. One of the objects which interested me most was a 'talking stick'. I bought one in a craft shop, and I recall the explanation offered to me by the shop owner as she was wrapping up my purchase.

'It's used in different ways throughout the indigenous cultures,' she said. 'When the tribal Council is deliberating on an important issue or deciding how to deal with a crisis, the talking stick is used to moderate the discussions. The stick is passed around the circle, and the person holding the talking stick is the only one who is permitted to speak. Everyone else listens. No interruption is allowed. So eventually everyone's viewpoint is heard – at least those who feel they have something useful to contribute. In the Great Councils, the Elders only make decisions after listening to all the viewpoints that are shared.'

I was fascinated – especially as I recalled some of the committees and groups I'd attended over the years which had descended into chaos as people talked over each other and tried to shout one another down to make sure their point of view prevailed. And I'd been in the chair often enough at such gatherings to know that moderating discussions among conflicting factions could be an

almost impossible task. But as we discussed the traditional pur-
poses and merits of the use of the talking stick, the shop owner
brought the whole concept into the present day.

'A talking stick can be used nowadays to help people connect
with each other,' she explained, 'to begin proper dialogue and to
come to a shared understanding through listening. It's amazing
what blessings people can find when they are prepared to listen
to one another.'

That statement has remained with me ever since.

It's amazing what blessings people can find
when they are prepared to listen to one another.

It came back to mind later in our trip when I spoke with a high
school teacher. When he heard about my talking stick and my
enthusiasm for the concepts behind its use, he was delighted to
tell me that he used one regularly in relationship-building and
conflict resolution in his school.

'It can be transformative,' he said, 'with groups or with two
people who are in some kind of conflict, because it creates a cli-
mate for good communication and teaches genuine listening
skills.' And he went on to outline a simple exercise he used.

'We begin with some quietish music. It settles things, creates a
reflective, calming atmosphere. We explain what we're going to
do then let the music run for a bit. After a minute or so, someone
gets the talking stick and has a whole sixty seconds to speak. The
other person or the rest of the group listens and doesn't interrupt.
After a minute, the facilitator – someone like me – dings a little
chime and the talking stick passes over to the other person or to
the next person in the group. And for another uninterrupted
minute that person has the chance to speak. And so it goes on.
Five minutes in total is usually enough for two people. It's longer
if it's a group. At the end – after another "ding" – someone takes

the talking stick and tries to summarise what has been said. If there's no summary possible, people are simply encouraged to stay in silence for a while to think about what has been shared. It's a great follow-up to a talk, or video, or lesson – or even a bust-up. Everyone gets to speak, and everyone gets to be heard.'

It's amazing what blessings people can find
when they are prepared to listen to one another.

'The talking stick,' the teacher concluded, 'is a tool for healing relationships and facilitating discussion and decision-making, speaking your truth and being listened to with respect.'

What a terrific idea! Even the quietest and most diffident voice can be heard. No one needs to be afraid that they won't be listened to. No one dominates a discussion.

This approach of encouraging gentle speaking and attentive listening is crucial at all levels of support for people who are bereaved. Bringing together people who are bereaved, for example, even for a short time, to explore their bereavement issues serves just this purpose.

I've spent many years facilitating bereavement support programmes. When I was part of the bereavement team in the hospice where I was chaplain, the support structure was built around small groups which met monthly. There were opportunities for one-to-one sharing too, of course, but group work was the foundation of the support offered to all the bereaved people cared for by the Marie Curie organisation in Edinburgh and the Lothians.

Since I retired from chaplaincy work, I have been offering group support through short bereavement support programmes (six weeks in duration) in Edinburgh (Acorns) and East Lothian (Stepping Stones). In coordinating and delivering these programmes, I've had countless experiences of the value of listening to people and allowing them the opportunity to tell their story.

The principle of such effective bereavement support – either in monthly groups or a programme which runs weekly for six weeks – is based on a 'talking stick approach', even if there isn't a physical talking stick to hand. The talking and sharing, the listening and affirming are crucial.

It's amazing what blessings people can find
when they are prepared to listen to one another.

In our bereavement groups – especially at the start when individuals are coming together for the first time – people have an opportunity to talk and be listened to in a way that previously might not have been possible for them. Even within the context of a loving, caring and supportive family, those who are bereaved can feel isolated and unheard in their grief. There is seldom malice in this, as it's often based on a genuine desire to be respectful and non-intrusive. But it can be very isolating, especially when people are first becoming aware of their bereavement issues and have no opportunity to articulate how they are feeling and what their questions might be.

Let me give you a personal example. My mother died at the age of fifty-eight. My father was still working and, though he lived with my sister, I knew how alone he felt after his wife's death. As had been my pattern for many years, I continued to phone him every Sunday evening to share the news of the week. Every time, at the beginning of the conversation, I would ask him how he was, and he would tell me he was fine. He would then ask me how I was, and I would tell him I was fine. And we would go on to talk about football, and the weather, and who had died in his village and – quite literally – the price of fish. As a caring son and a caring father, we'd done our job and asked after each other's welfare. And by saying we were 'fine', we were giving a signal that we wanted to move on with our conversation and get to safer and less emotional ground. But I would sometimes end the phone call in tears. And my dad would sometimes end the phone call in tears. How did we know this? Because my sister and my wife 'grassed' on us. They knew how we *really* felt and how we were coping, while all the time my dad and I were choosing to hide it from each other.

A father and son couldn't be truly honest because each was more concerned about the other than they were about themselves. We were being respectful, protective, non-intrusive. We were being the father and son we'd always been to one another. I didn't want to tell my dad I was having a hard time or a bad week because to do so might have made things worse for him. Then he might have worried more about me than he needed to do about himself. So I kept my feelings to myself because I cared so much for him. But that only served to increase *my* isolation – and his too, I learned – and to diminish opportunities for genuine sharing and openness.

I know now what I didn't know then, that this is extremely common. The language of grief is often so inadequate, and the opportunities to be genuinely open and understanding with one another so limited, that we resort to clichés. 'I'm fine ...' 'Not too bad ...' 'Ups and downs ...' 'Getting there ...' become code phrases for: 'Thanks for asking, but I can't tell you more, and anyway I suspect you're not prepared to listen. And, even if you are, I'm not sure I could cope with making things worse for you.'

In recent times I've worked with several widows and widowers whose life-partners have died at an unnaturally young age, leaving them as single parents to bring up little children. Their bereavements all followed a similar pattern. Each of them took on the role of what they believed was expected of them as a parent – protecting their children from pain; offering appropriate nurture; giving themselves totally to their children's well-being. Some of them encouraged their children to talk, and intuitively had the right approach and appropriate skills. Others sought help and guidance – through books, online resources and caring agencies – to develop appropriate skills and confidence to help their children through their loss. But *all* of them, without exception, told the same kind of story and shared the same kind of anxieties about their own grief and journey of loss.

'Who listens to me?'

'If I cry in front of the children it'll make it worse for them.'

'I'm exhausted keeping up for the little ones. I just collapse when they go to bed.'

'I feel my whole life is given to their welfare; I have no time for myself.'

'Where do *I* go to say that life is crap?'

'Who the hell will bother with me?'

Of course, in individual circumstances such statements can be challenged and better strategies developed. But such cries of pain – for that is what they are – all come from that common place of isolation and the familiar, heart-rending question: 'Where can I tell my story as it really is?'

One young widow expressed it this way: 'For months after my husband died, I took the role – and I fulfilled it well – of a single parent, a mother to two young children whose father had been taken from us. It took me ages to realise that I was also a grieving widow. My husband had died, not just the father of my children. I listened to my little ones and encouraged them to be open and honest about their loss. But then I began to realise that no one was listening to me.'

When I was a parish minister and a funeral director phoned to ask if I was available to conduct a local funeral, usually all the information I was given was the name and age of the deceased, the family's address and phone number, the next-of-kin's details, and a little – often very little indeed – about the person who had died or the nature of the death. I would arrange to visit the bereaved family at a mutually convenient time to begin to plan the funeral, and when I went to the home I would always say something like, 'Tell me about John' or 'Was the death sudden or had Annie been ill for a while?' or 'How are things with you?' Then I would get the *whole* story.

Sometimes it would be long and complicated. Occasionally it would be incredibly traumatic – such as a suicide, or a car accident, or a violent death. Often it contained lots of irrelevant background and unnecessary information. But *always* it was a story people needed to tell – to hear themselves articulate things, often for the first time; to explore their issues, often for the only time; but, above all, to be listened to, often at the most important time.

If you take that forward a few months beyond the time of the funeral, perhaps well into the first year of the loss, you can understand what might be happening. The immediate impact of the death has dissipated. People no longer ask how you are – or even express sympathy. Interest in listening to your story has waned. Even if you had the opportunity to tell your story at the start, all too soon people give you signals that they don't want to hear it again. If you have offered indications that you're coping, all too quickly people give you the impression that they're not particularly interested in hearing that you're no longer coping well.

So, when people have the opportunity to be together in their bereavements, through that first year of grief and loss but also well beyond, listening is all the more important. Moreover, it often takes place outside the family circle where they have the freedom to be themselves and not worry about anyone else.

The talking stick issue is this: bereaved people need to talk and to be listened to in an environment of understanding and empathy that is accepting and non-judgemental. How often people have said to us: 'The most important thing about sharing with each other is that people nod. No one interrupts. You're given space and time to try to put into words the important bits of the story. Nods help so much with that.'

They have been given a metaphorical talking stick, and they know that others are genuinely listening to them.

It's amazing what blessings people can find
when they are prepared to listen to one another.

The effect of this is emphasised when someone has a difficult part of their story to tell. In one of our bereavement groups in the hospice we had Trevor, a young gay man, whose partner had died in his mid-fifties from bowel cancer. They weren't in a civil partnership or a marriage (it was before the legislation for such things was in place) so he had no official or legal status after his partner's death. He was 'just a good friend', and yet he was, of course, devastated by the death of the most important person in his life.

Trevor articulated his story in the group in a gentle, dignified and tearful fashion, and if there were any prejudices about gay relationships, we never saw them. If there was any judgement about the loss of 'just a good friend', it was never evident. Instead, what we got were nods, quiet listening, sensitive expressions of understanding and comments which served to draw out more of the story and the feelings he needed to express. This was all because people could feel for Trevor's sorrow from the similar journeys of grief they were travelling themselves.

We begin to understand the feelings of others when we recognise them as our own. I remember Monica coming to the first meeting of one of our Acorns support programmes. In her forties, she was clearly nervous, and it didn't take much to work out that she'd been crying before she came into the room. We made her feel as much at home as we could, took time to share tea and coffee together, introduced her to the team and some of the other participants, and in time settled down with her round a table to begin our session. The opening session of our six-week programmes is always the most emotional, as people are encouraged to share why they have come along and something of their loss and circumstances. There are always lots of tears – and, thankfully, lots of nods too – as people take the opportunity to tell as much of their story as they choose. No one is forced to speak. Some have a lot to say; some can't say much because of tears; some struggle to say anything at all. But it quickly becomes clear that honesty in our sharing is why we're together, and that there is benefit to everyone if folk can be open with and respectful of one another. So in our group the talking stick was metaphorically passed around, and the sharing began.

Through it all, as several people shared some of their story, Monica studiously kept her eyes on the table, avoiding eye-contact with me and everyone else. In a group of ten people, five or six had already spoken when Monica suddenly lifted her head, flushed scarlet, looked straight at me, and said quietly, 'Can I speak next?'

'Of course,' I responded.

Then, concentrating once more on the table-top, she said in a gentle but shaking voice, 'My husband took his own life ... three months ago ... pills and whisky in a hotel room ... he was forty-eight ... his name was Terry ...'

It was as much as she could say. She broke down in tears. There was a collective intake of breath from the others. Some of the group were crying. I was just about to break the silence, when the woman sitting next to Monica got there before me, blurting out, 'My God! Me too!'

It was the first time this woman had contributed, and, putting her hand on Monica's forearm, she continued, 'My husband committed suicide too, six months ago, from a bridge, and I'm sitting here terrified that I wouldn't be able to say that.'

'What was his name?' Monica asked through her tears.

'Victor,' the woman replied. 'He was fifty-nine.'

If there had been an intake of breath at Monica's revelation, there was a deep, collective sigh with this new story. Two women sharing painful, traumatic accounts of their bereavement had found common ground. But much more than that, they had found a listening forum with others who could relate to the pain of their loss because of their own emotions and struggles, even though their losses were not considered so traumatic. The talking stick had done its job, and the foundation of an open, honest and understanding sharing had been established to underpin the unfolding of the programme over subsequent weeks.

The issues thrown up by a death – whether sudden or predictable, traumatic or straightforward, involving old or young, gay or straight, or a variety of relationships including 'just a good friend' – exhibit more common ground than anyone ever expects. But how are people going to know that unless they have an opportunity to share and 'check things out' with others? All the more reason for people to be given a talking stick in their bereavements, and for the rest of us to take time to listen, and to listen again, when nods communicate much more understanding than 'How are you?' and 'I'm fine' can ever do.

Listening, however, isn't just about having the opportunity to share the difficult parts of the story, important though that obviously is. It's about creating an opportunity to listen to the 'successes' as well, no matter how trivial or strange such signs of progress might seem.

By any measurement, Walter was not only finding the sharing in our bereavement programme of value, he was also communicating that he was coping well. But there was one indication of 'moving forward' that he couldn't share in the group but needed to reveal in private with someone he trusted. On this occasion, I was the one who had the opportunity to listen.

'Can I have a word?' he asked me as people were leaving at the end of a group session. 'There's something I need to tell you.'

I expected to hear of a problem or a difficult aspect of the loss of his wife he hadn't been able to share with the whole group. We found a quiet corner, and I asked him what his issue was. He took me completely by surprise when he said, 'I've got myself a tattoo.'

'Oh!' I replied, not really knowing what else I was expected to say.

Appreciating my mild discomfort, Walter continued, 'Evelyn didn't like tattoos, even though I'd talked about getting one for years. So, for forty-three years of our marriage getting a tattoo was a no-no. But now, nine months after she died, I decided I needed to do something for me, as a sign, I suppose, that it's my life and my future I've to take care of now. So, I got myself a tattoo. It's got an E in it for the love of my life, and an open book because she was a writer.' I nodded, because I still didn't know how else to respond. Walter nodded too. 'Now, don't go asking me where it is, because I might have to tell you. But I just needed you to know it's been done. My tattoo is my symbol of moving on.'

I shook Walter by the hand and simply said, 'Thank you.' He'd trusted me with an important part of his story. I'd been prepared to listen, and that had been enough. Once more, the talking stick had done its job.

It's amazing what blessings people can find
when they are prepared to listen to one another.

If we are to offer constructive support to those who are bereaved, we have to begin by listening to their story. If bereaved people are to access the care and understanding they crave in their journeys of loss, they need to know that there are people out there who are prepared to listen, and to listen some more, when other ears have been closed and the voices of bereaved people are prematurely silenced.

Listening

I listened with my ears;
it's what you do with ears;
it's what they were made for;
and someone was speaking.
So, I listened with my ears,
in case there was something important to hear.

I listened with my eyes;
you can do that with eyes;
they can see things people say
when words aren't enough.
So, I listened with my eyes
in case there was something important to heed.

I listened with my mind;
you can think when you're listening
about 'Whys' and 'Hows'
as you try to understand.
So, I listened with my mind,
in case there was something important to grasp.

I listened with my experience;
'empathy' they say it's called.
I tried hard to find a new way in
to what was shared.
So, I listened with my experience,
in case there was something important to feel.

I listened with my ears
and my eyes
and my mind

and my experience,
and I began to hear
and heed
and grasp
and feel
an unfolding story.

I listened ...
and I heard ...

and I hadn't said anything yet.

Chapter 2

The uniqueness of loss

My first car was a Ford Anglia. It had belonged to my sister for several years and to our uncle before that, so it was a fair age when I got it. But it was all I could afford, and as a trainee minister on a low wage, living alone and with no responsibilities to transport other people here and there, it served me just fine. Being far from new it was, not surprisingly, far from perfect. But its many idiosyncrasies made it unique. And I loved my old car!

It had a front-wheel wobble when it touched 55mph – not at 50, mind you – and by the time you pushed the accelerator pedal to the floor and were racing along at 60, the wobble had disappeared. I don't know if every Ford Anglia had a wheel-wobble at 55mph, but mine did, and I loved the individuality of it.

The driver's door wouldn't open from the inside. You could get *in* OK, but decanting consisted of an undignified clamber over the gear-lever and handbrake and out through the passenger door. It wasn't the kind of car you exited from quickly, that's for sure.

Sometimes it wouldn't start. That was usually because the bolts which fixed the starter-motor to the engine block had worked themselves loose and the gearing of the starter had failed to engage with the engine's fly-wheel. Problematic? Not at all. All that was needed was for the driver to switch on the ignition, lean into the engine and hold the starter-motor hard against the engine casing, press a rubber ignition button just under the bonnet, and the engine would jump into life. It never failed. It was a theft-preventing immobiliser long before electronic versions came into vogue.

The nearside front wing had been so rusted it was patched up with chicken-wire and filler. And did I say that the passenger seat didn't tip forward far enough to allow easy access into the back?

But this car was mine! Lovable, unique, idiosyncratic, it was mine! My car may have been different from other cars, perhaps from every other Ford Anglia, but I knew all its ways and that was all that mattered.

Well, that *should* have been all that mattered until I started going out with Mary, the young woman who was to become my wife … and all through our engagement, and into the first couple of years of our marriage. What was personal to *me*, I now had to explain to someone else. The idiosyncrasies I had learned to live with that I'd never needed to share with anyone now had to be elaborated on and excused. My relationship with the uniqueness of my old Anglia now had to be scrutinised by another interested and involved party.

It wasn't that I was unwilling to share my secrets with Mary. It's just that I was embarrassed by having to talk about, and help *her* live with, the quirkiness and individuality of my car. To be honest, finding the words to do that seemed very strange.

This is a metaphor for another important issue in bereavement – the very difficult process of having to explain things we have never had to put into words before. It's all very well having a talking stick and finding the opportunity to speak. It's quite something else to use that opportunity to articulate ideas and concepts you've never needed or been able to verbalise before.

Any relationship we have in life – between parent and child, siblings, friends or life-partners – is unique to the two people who are involved. Whether that relationship is long-term or relatively new, it is founded on two people committing to it openly, honestly and completely, such that the bond grows and deepens. And, of course, in the uniqueness of that interconnection, there are always idiosyncrasies that are personal, distinctive and private. That's what makes loving relationships so very special and important.

My wife and I have nicknames for each other. No one, after more than forty years of our marriage, knows what they are. They don't need to. Our nicknames are personal and quirky. They are unique to our relationship. To explain them to anyone else would, frankly, be embarrassing. That's why we keep them private. And I'm certainly not going to reveal them here …

It's not just about names either. It's about things we do together. For example, through all our married life we have always slept on our 'own side' of a double bed. Even when sleeping alone, we always sleep on the side that we're used to.

Do nicknames and what side of the bed we sleep on really matter? Not to anyone else in the whole world. But they do to us, because, along with many other intimacies, they make our relationship unique and personal to the two of us. We're the only people who are involved, the only ones who need to know. But what I am sure of is this: when one of us dies and leaves the other behind, our nicknames will die too; and when the bereaved partner continues sleeping in the marital bed – if that is what they choose to do – they will almost certainly keep sleeping on the same side and will desperately miss the person who has lain beside them for so many years. Is it any wonder that widows and widowers tells us how hard it is in the early stage of bereavement to go to bed alone, or to wake up in the morning and realise again that the bed is empty?

If every relationship is unique, and if that uniqueness – such as my loving relationship with my Anglia – is built on and strengthened by many shared and understood idiosyncrasies, then it's not surprising that when someone is bereaved, all the private intimacies, all the bits and pieces that went to make up the uniqueness, die too.

So, how do we find words to express what that means to us in our journey of loss? How do we talk about and explain things we have never had to put into words before? Is it any surprise that we find that process so very hard and painful?

I worked with an elderly gentleman who, following a group support session, asked me if he could speak privately as there was something he couldn't share in the group. Dennis had been married to his late wife, Emily, for fifty-nine years. For almost a decade he had been her carer as he nurtured – and then nursed – her through the debilitating effects of Alzheimer's. For the six months before she died, she'd been in a nursing home and Dennis had visited her faithfully twice a day. She didn't know him. He was weary with his caring. He prayed she would die.

In time, she did. Dennis had told us in the group sessions that he was relieved. She was 'out of her suffering', he said, and to an extent, he had to admit, so was he. He'd lost his wife. And he had rationalised, well enough, what that meant. But what he wasn't prepared for was the loss of everything that went with the death of his wife, all the intimacies and idiosyncrasies that made his relationship with her unique.

Bereavement is not about a single loss – the loss of the person – though that's generally all people know about and concentrate on. Dennis had also lost his routine; his purpose in life; his role; his focus; and much more besides. He could be open about *some* of that in the group, of course, because it was largely safe stuff and easy enough for others to understand and relate to. And, indeed, there were people in that particular group who had similar stories to tell. He was good at sharing, articulated well, took on board comments and suggestions and listened to and was supportive of others in the group. So, what might he need to talk about on his own, I wondered.

It was quite specific, I discovered, and when we sat together over coffee in his home, he got around to it quite quickly. 'It's about sex,' he said. 'I've been having dreams about Emily, and my dreams are not about her being old, or about her time in the care home, or about her death. I might have expected that. But they're about sex, and what we got up to many, many years ago.' He smiled. 'I'll not reveal the details about *that*,' he affirmed, 'but I just needed to tell you about my dreams, and to ask you if they're OK.'

Of course they were OK, and I don't need to say here how the conversation continued. But what matters is that here was an intimacy – a part of his story and his journey of bereavement – that was deeply private and distinctive, that he needed to share and clarify, and at least try to put into words to help him make sense of it all. In short, he was having to explain the individuality of his Ford Anglia for the very first time.

When I worked in the hospice, I was asked by the son of one of the patients who had recently died if I could be in touch with his mother as he was worried about how she was coping in the first few weeks of her loss. I enquired whether he'd asked her if it was OK for me to contact her. 'No,' he said, 'I just told her you would.'

So, with some reluctance and not a little apprehension, I phoned the lady and gently enquired as to how things were. 'I was just thinking about you,' I lied … 'so I thought I'd give you a ring.'

I knew her well, so it wasn't a surprise to her that I was in touch to ask after her welfare. She started to cry early in our conversation, and cried a lot, on and off, as we talked. There were some long pauses too while she sought to compose herself. 'I know my son thinks I'm going nuts because I cry so much,' she said.

'Remind me how long it is since your husband died,' I asked at one point.

'Seven weeks,' she replied. We agreed that, in this relatively short time-frame, tears were not only appropriate, but also helpful in the bereavement process. If she cried on the phone, I suggested, it was probably because she spent so much energy hiding her tears from her son and the rest of the family. Crying was a positive thing.

'What's the worst bit of the day?' I asked.

Long pause ... more tears ... 'Going to bed,' she responded.

'Do you have a photo of your husband on your bedside table?'

Longer pause ... more tears ... 'Yes, I do.'

'I'll bet you kiss him goodnight before you put the light out.'

Another long pause ... even more tears ... 'Yes, every night.'

'And sometimes you put his photo under your pillow so that you can be as close to him as possible while you're asleep?'

Longest pause ... but no tears ... deep sigh ... followed by a gentle question: 'How did you know that? Have you been looking through my bedroom window?'

'No,' I replied. 'But it's what people do.'

Another long pause ... and I detected a smile through the tears. 'If that's the case you'll not be surprised to know that I wear his jammies in bed too, because I get the smell of him ...'

Intimacies? Of course. And a reassurance that there is no madness there. Differences? Yes. Common ground with others? That too, I reassured her. But in being allowed to 'tell it as it is' and finding acceptance in that, the uniqueness of the relationship and the individuality of what the bereavement journey meant for this individual were suitably affirmed.

I'm not saying that this conversation with a grieving widow seven weeks after her husband had died somehow magically sorted everything out for the remainder of her bereavement journey. But I *am* saying that sharing some of the intimacies of loss might have given her clues about one aspect of bereavement that she could usefully explore further.

How many times have people shared their own intimacies with us, the little things that reinforce, often very painfully, the loneliness and isolation of their loss? The times when someone will turn to another to comment about something that took their fancy on the TV, only to be struck again by the painful truth that the person with whom they'd shared such intimacies over many years isn't there any more …

The times when a son will continue to shout 'Coooeee, mum,' when he comes home from work only to realise, once again, that his mother isn't there to respond with a welcoming, 'How are you, son?'

The times when a special brand of cheese is thrown into a shopping trolley 'because it's the kind William likes best', only to be reminded when the shopping is being unpacked that William isn't there to enjoy it.

The times when a daughter picks up the phone to call her mother to ask for her special recipe for Dundee Cake only to remember that there will never be that kind of conversation again.

The times when this writer is reduced to tears in church because *Be thou my vision* has been chosen as one of the hymns – his father's favourite, sung during the War, used at his funeral – and no one else knows why.

There is private hurt and sorrow in grief: the brokenness that comes from intimacies, deeply and lovingly shared, and painfully remembered; the loss of all that has been poured into the uniqueness of a relationship with someone you have loved in a special way.

When Prince Albert, the husband and consort of Queen Victoria, died in 1861, he and the Queen had been married for just over twenty years. He was 42 when he died, and it is well documented that his death plunged Queen Victoria into deep mourning.

Not long after she and Albert had met, and reflecting on the prospect of marriage, the young Victoria had written to her uncle Leopold to thank him 'for the prospect of great happiness you have contributed to give me in the person of dear Albert … He possesses every quality that could be desired to render me perfectly happy.'[1]

But Victoria's 'great happiness' had been shattered by Albert's untimely death. Her descent into a crippling state of unrelenting grief rapidly created problems for those who were concerned for her and anxious about her ability to concentrate on and deal with her 'affairs of state'. It soon became clear that Victoria's retreat from public view and her intense sorrow would endure well beyond the usual two years of conventional mourning. Without Albert she felt rudderless. To lose him, as she herself said, was 'like tearing the flesh from my bones'. The isolation of her position as queen was profound. 'There is no one to call me Victoria now,' she wept, in response to the grinding loss of intimacy, affection and physical love she now felt.[2]

There is no one to call me Victoria now is a telling cry of sorrow and despair. The public face of the monarch would be 'Your majesty', 'Ma'am', and the like. But the private face, the intimacy of her relationship with Albert, was symbolised by the need to be called Victoria, the need to be loved in a unique and special fashion.

In my parish ministry and hospice chaplaincy I was often invited to officiate at funerals. This is not a place to share how a funeral is co-created between officiant and family, but it is important to say that the creation of a funeral that works as a platform for the next stage of the bereavement process is as taxing as it is important. Such a process is based on honesty and openness, so that the funeral can be tailored to suit the needs of the grieving family and as a fitting tribute to the person who has died.

I have often described a funeral as a bridge, something designed to help bereaved people cross the chasm from what has been known and familiar to the unknown and uncharted territory of bereavement. If that bridge is shaky – in other words, if the funeral doesn't work well – uncertain people will step off the bridge having had a scary and unsound crossing. But if the funeral has been a good experience, then no matter how fearful people might be about stepping into the new and strange world of loss, they will at least have the opportunity to step off the bridge with a degree of confidence.

I worked closely with a craggy old retired miner when I was in the hospice. Peter was a Communist and not great with any religion. The only reason that he and I had got on so well is that I quickly realised I was on the coat-tails of ministers and priests he'd known who'd stood by miners and their families during the devastation of the miners' strikes in the 1980s. Because of their work and standing in mining communities, Peter had decided that I was one of 'the good guys'! During one of our lengthy conversations, he asked me if I would conduct his funeral when it was his time. I told him it would be a privilege. And that's the way we left things.

When it came time to arrange the funeral, I sat with Jessie, his widow, in the privacy of a hospice room, and we started to plan things. She said how surprised she was that Peter would have had anything to do with the likes of me, far less ask me to officiate at his funeral. When we got to the stage of preparing a brief tribute to her husband, I asked her if she could describe him to me and say a little of what he meant to her. She smiled.

'He was a bastard,' she said.

Not surprisingly, I was taken aback by the honesty and graphic nature of her words. She clocked that and smiled more broadly.

'For eighty per cent of his life he was a bastard,' she continued. 'Drink, language, more time with "comrades" and union officials than with me. Oh, I could give as good as I got, but there were times when it was hellish. For twenty per cent of his life he was wonderful – which is why I stayed with him all those years.'

It was my turn to smile. 'I'm not sure I can say that in a tribute,' I suggested.

'Oh I know *that*,' Jessie continued. 'But I just needed you to know what kind of man we're dealing with here.'

Jessie had had a Ford Anglia of a husband that she'd learned to live with – a man she'd loved and hated in imbalanced proportions for many years. But now she had to find words to explain what the reality of her man *actually* was. And she'd done so with absolute honesty and devastating openness.

Of course, I didn't include 'Peter was a bastard' as part of the funeral tribute. I remember using phrases such as 'He was a man of many facets' and 'Like us all, Peter had his good side and his not-so-good side,' and seeing nods and smiles of acknowledgement from the mourners. An intimacy had been revealed in the privacy of a supportive conversation, and I suspect that, for Jessie, this had been hard. But it was enough. She had acknowledged the uniqueness of their relationship in an appropriate way, and now she needed to leave it at that.

If I were as honest as Jessie, I would have to say that my beloved Ford Anglia was a bastard at times too. And the percentage of that? I think that will have to remain suitably private for now.

As a hospice chaplain I was told that part of my role was to help people 'articulate their longings'. That is emphasised all the more in the uniqueness of every loss, where opportunities for the articulation of the individuality of grief and the personal dimensions of bereavement are sadly lacking. So let's encourage people to be honest, even when that's hard, and to find words to express their deepest longings, even though they might never have been able to before. And, you never know, as someone finds an articulation of their feelings with you, then you might also be able to begin that process of discovery for yourself.

Missing you

I miss you in the morning when you wake me up real slow
with a cup of tea in bed at half-past eight.
I miss you in the evening when I have to lock the doors
and I'm tired and find it hard to concentrate.
I miss you when I've lost the number of the local Vet,
and I need to get advice about the cat.
I miss you, how I miss you, in those moments that we shared …
But who is going to listen to all *that*?

I miss you when I prowl along the aisles in *B&Q*
and I'm checking colour-charts all on my own.
I miss you when I don't know how to reinsure the car
and I've lost the charger for my mobile phone.
I miss you watching *Strictly* even though it's not your scene;
I even miss your banter and chit-chat.
I miss you, how I miss you, in those silly little times …
But who is going to listen to all *that*?

I miss you when the news is on the telly and you say,
'Just what *is* that politician saying now?'
I miss the David Attenborough DVDs we watched,
and the way you said, 'How wonderful!' or 'Wow!'
I miss you when I comment and you're not there to respond,
or when I make a joke and it falls flat.
I miss you, how I miss you, in those secret, private ways …
But who is going to listen to all *that*?

I miss you when the brochures for the holidays arrive
and I have to make another bloody choice.
I miss you when I'm lonely, and I fear I'm going mad
when I speak to you and think I hear your voice.

So if I'm going to miss you like I miss you every day,
there's something that I might just dabble at ...
I miss you ... so I'll *tell* you that I miss you when I do.
'Cause *you're* the one who'll understand all *that*!

1. Stanley Weintraub, *Albert: Uncrowned King*, 1997, p 51
2. http://www.historyextra.com/period/victorian/prince-albert-the-death-that-rocked-the-monarchy/

Chapter 3

Looking good for the photo

Hanging in the hallway of my home there's a studio photograph of my late father's family. My father was one of eight children, raised in a two-roomed tenement property in Fort William in the highlands of Scotland. His father died when he was seven years old leaving his mother to bring up her family, ranging in age from six months to fourteen years, in relative poverty. Over the next few years this hard-working and caring woman wore herself out working to make sure her children did more than merely survive. And she did well, for her eight offspring were a credit to her and, in their own way, continued her legacy of hard work, family commitment and righteous living. My father was fourteen when she died.

The photograph I've inherited isn't the complete family, showing only six of the eight children, as the younger siblings, Ewan and Catherine, were born later. The youngest at the time, my uncle Donald, is a baby on his mother's knee; the other children – John, Alexander, Hugh, Jessie and James (my dad) – are ranged behind; and the imposing and dignified figure of their father stands at the back, watchful and proud.

This post-Victorian, posed, studio study would have been a major expense for a working-class family, and so it clearly mattered a great deal. My grandfather is in his Sunday best. My grandmother appears calm, almost serene. All the children are scrubbed and well presented, including my father – aged about three – smartly turned out in a fetching white polo-necked sweater.

There is, however, a story behind the picture which my father delighted in telling. On the morning of the day on which the photograph was to be taken, the children had been well warned to behave, to keep themselves out of mischief and, above all, to stay *clean*! Somehow, however, my father managed to escape, and found himself in Fort William High Street where some workmen were busy repairing the road. A key element of their work was a massive tar boiler. The inevitable happened, and when my father was eventually rescued from his newly-discovered play-area, the front of his pristine white sweater was covered in spots of black tar. There were ructions, of course, and his mother would, by then, have been far from calm and serene. But there clearly wasn't time to find new clothes (even if there were any) for a recalcitrant child in preparation for the important photograph. So, an ever-resourceful mother did the simplest and most effective thing she could think of – she took off the tar-stained sweater, turned it around, and plonked it back over the head of my (presumably) contrite father so that he was now wearing the white sweater back-to-front. The offending tar stains were out of sight. The clean part of the sweater was all that could be seen. My father looked terrific from the front, as if nothing untoward had happened – and that was good enough for the photograph.

A three-year-old boy, looking solid, dependable and extremely well-behaved in a family studio-portrait photograph, is *actually* wearing his sweater the wrong way round so that it looks good for the picture, with the mess he'd made well out of sight. Looking at the picture now, no one would know what trauma had preceded the taking of that photograph, the tears and the panic affecting everyone just a few moments before the camera-shutter clicked.

People who are bereaved are often like my father in that family photograph. They try to present, as much as they are able, a clean, tidy, well-managed image to the rest of the world, while out of sight there is the damage, hurt, tears, confusion and distress that most of us never get to know about, stains on their image that they choose, mostly, not to reveal.

Twenty-five years ago, a good friend and colleague in the ministry died suddenly and unexpectedly. The news of his death was devastating for all those who knew and respected a fine man and an excellent parish minister. Members of his congregation were naturally overwhelmed and distressed. The day after his death, I met one of his senior elders. Donald was in his seventies and had been very close to his minister, and as we sympathised with each other and talked about our friend, we were both close to tears. Then I realised that Donald, out shopping for his daily paper and morning rolls, was wearing his dark Sunday suit, a white shirt and black tie. He told me that this is what he had been wearing since he heard the news of his minister's death. And he would wear it to the funeral, and probably for some time beyond.

'I need people to know I am in mourning,' he told me, 'and how important my minister was to me.'

In the intervening twenty years since my friend's death, this reaction has become rare. People like Donald are now few and far between. Long gone are the days when 'widow's weeds', for example, would be the common mode of dress for a year and a day for a woman in mourning following the death of her husband. We have moved well past an era when people would dress themselves in various shades of grey to indicate that they were still close to the time of their loss. And to bring things right up to date, how infrequent has black become as the chosen, respectful style of dress at a funeral, whether by the personal request of the immediate family or the individual choice of some mourners? What would old Donald make of that, I wonder?

Comments such as 'Bert wouldn't have liked us to be sad', and 'It's about celebration and not mourning for Anne' encourage family mourners and grieving friends to wear brighter clothes, or, at the very least, not to dress sombrely. Instructions in obituary notices to funeral attendees such as 'No black, please' or even 'Please wear green and white because that was his football club's colours' often define the approach that's expected of those in mourning. In effect, bereaved people try their best – and are frequently expected – to look good for the photograph and present themselves well to the rest of the world.

We know societal norms change over time. Donald was an old man, a product of the received social expectations of a past generation. But it shouldn't be assumed that if people take a different approach to his that they are being any less respectful or that they are not grieving in an appropriate way. There are many positives in families taking ownership of the style and content of a funeral, for example. But it's my experience that this has the potential to create problems in the grieving process.

Far too soon, people are expected to 'get back to normal' after a death. When we are bereaved, people in our street, village, community, church, club, school, workplace, or the like, very quickly forget that we have had major loss in our lives. Within too narrow a time-frame, people expect us to wear our white polo-necked sweater back-to-front as we pose for the photographer and try to look our best in society's studio.

My father died twenty years after my mother. He was still living in Fort William, while I had been based in Edinburgh with my own family for many years. He was eighty-two when his full and loving life came to its end and he slipped away quietly in the nursing home where he'd stayed for a short time prior to his death. I was better prepared for my father's death than I had been for my mother's twenty years before, because I was more familiar with, and understanding of, the journey of bereavement. With hindsight, however, I know that I made one major mistake.

When I was making the arrangements for his funeral, I had to decide which newspaper I should use for his obituary notice. I chose the Aberdeen-based *Press & Journal*, the closest equivalent to a standard daily paper for the highlands of Scotland. Given that the funeral was ten days away, I also put the notice in the weekly *Oban Times*, the most widely read paper in the Lochaber area. And, in typical local fashion, black-bordered funeral notices, prepared by the funeral director, also appeared in various locations in Fort William and around the area, designed to spread as quickly and widely as possible the news of his death to anyone who would be interested in attending the funeral. What I chose *not* to do, however, was to put a corresponding obituary notice in an Edinburgh-based newspaper. No one knew my dad in Edinburgh. My family, work colleagues and friends were all up to speed with things through personal contact with me. No newspaper announcement to give them the appropriate information was necessary. And, to be honest, I didn't want to draw attention to myself and my loss. So I decided there was no need for a notice of my father's death in *The Scotsman* or Edinburgh's *Evening News*.

When I got back to Edinburgh after the funeral and for some time thereafter, no one outwith my immediate family, circle of friends and work colleagues in the hospice was aware that I was in mourning. I wasn't old Donald. I wore no black. I didn't have a big neon sign over my head announcing, 'Please be patient with this man. He's recently lost his father.'

Ten days after the funeral, I went back to work in the hospice. I sat at the bedsides of people who were dying. I gave off whatever signals I could that all was well. In short, I had begun – so very quickly – to wear my polo-necked sweater back-to-front for the photographs. I wanted to portray a positive image. How could I support people who were dying or recently bereaved if they saw weakness in me, if they were disturbed by tar stains on my pristine white sweater?

But there was a problem with people 'not knowing'. I found myself pushed further and further into the 'pretending' role, acting the part, wearing the mask. My presentation for the 'photograph' was the cheery, confident, strong, caring, 'together' image that people were familiar with. My sweater stayed back-to-front. Only the good side was on show. However, it didn't always work.

I remember going to a big church meeting about a month after my father's death. It was what is known in the Church of Scotland as a 'Presbytery' gathering – a meeting of ministers and others from all over the city to deal with the business of the Church of Scotland in Edinburgh and its environs. As was typical at such gatherings, a tribute had been paid to a retired minister who had recently died. I'd known Matthew for many years, and I'd looked to him often for advice and guidance in my early years of ministry. He was someone I considered a good role-model. I was feeling weary and down but, as usual, I was trying to hide it. A colleague spoke to me as we were leaving the meeting, clearly expecting me to be the bright, cheerful chap I usually was.

'You're looking a bit tired,' she remarked.

I blurted out. 'Oh, it's Matthew's death, I suppose.' I paused, not really knowing what to say next, and then, before I knew it, I'd added, 'And just after my father's death too.' In an instant, my colleague's attitude changed. She'd found the tar stains on the back of my sweater, the damage I had inadvertently revealed.

'Oh, Tom, I am *so* sorry. I didn't know …' My mask had slipped, and there was unwanted fuss, and emotion, and … I couldn't wait to get home.

I've heard many similar stories. Bereaved people find it hard to be 'out and about' after a death. 'People don't know what to say,' they tell me, 'so I see them avoiding me, or I just try to avoid them.' They tell me it's hard enough when people *know* what's happened and don't know what to say or do. But how much harder it is when people *don't* know about the loss and expect the person who is bereaved to be the same person they've always been. On those occasions, someone who is hurting sore – and who is aware of the tar stains they're trying to hide – struggles to maintain their presentable, good-side-to-the-camera image and is all the more distressed when they don't succeed.

When I was a young minister, I worked with a couple who'd had four children. The eldest, a nineteen-year-old-daughter who had three younger brothers, had died of leukaemia some years before. When I first met them, I asked – as you do – what family they had. 'Four children,' the father said, 'a girl and three boys.' It was some time before I learned the whole story. He talked as though the family was still complete – which, in his mind, it clearly was. But at that point he couldn't, or wouldn't, indicate to this new minister anything of the loss he'd experienced. It was some months – and even then it was incredibly hard – before a father could talk with his minister about a daughter who had died.

So, whether you're in the baked-beans aisle in Sainsbury's and meet someone you know, or you're interacting with strangers in a social setting, or even talking to a sympathetic minister who is seeking to get to know you better, when your loss *is* revealed – especially when you would rather it hadn't been – it can be very difficult indeed.

What, then, are we to do? Wear our tar-stained sweater with a 'What the hell?' attitude, not caring how it might look in the family photograph? Get a big sign (like one of those forlorn people who stand on the street corners of our towns with a big arrow on top of a long pole indicating that a 'Golf Sale' or 'Pizza Parlour' is just a few yards away) to carry around to indicate to all and sundry that we are bereaved, so that everyone knows and can react accordingly? Well possibly, and this is what some bereaved people try to do. But, to be honest, I've not come across many people who can carry it off – me included – even though there's a part of us which may feel that it would be the better way.

We are left, therefore, to our own devices or our personal choices, expending time and energy hiding our tar stains from the photographer and looking good for the picture. And that's OK. It really is. Nowadays, it's a reasonable way to function – both for ourselves, and for the people we bump into at a church meeting or in the ready-meals section of our local supermarket.

We can't live with tears all the time. We must go about our daily living, interact with others and create normality for ourselves. We know what we're doing, and it's OK. The bottom line is that it allows us to function. But we also have to learn, or at least *try* to learn, that it is OK to live in the *other* world at the same time. We can live in two worlds simultaneously: the world of coping – showing our good side – and the world of struggling – the tar stains on our lovely sweater.

In the mid-90s, Margaret Stroebe and Henk Schut presented a theory of grief called the *Dual Process Model*. This bereavement theory suggests that grief operates in two main ways, and people switch back and forth between them as they grieve. Stroebe and Schut made it clear that, in all losses, both expressing and controlling feelings are equally important, and that normal grief sees the bereaved person oscillating between coping behaviours. This is the 'living in two worlds' concept. Bereaved people find that going between them is not only normal but absolutely necessary.

Of course, the degree and emphasis of the oscillation will vary from person to person, depending on individual life and environmental factors and over different time scales. But the truth is this: by taking time off from the pain of grief a bereaved person may be more able to cope with their daily life and the dramatic changes it has undergone.

There is, of course, the danger that bereaved people – myself included – don't give themselves permission to slip back into the world of grieving after they have lived for a time in the world of coping.

When I conducted my first cot-death funeral, my new baby daughter was six months old. My identification with a grieving family was total and I hoped I would be able to conduct the funeral service with enough dignity and purpose that it was helpful to them. And I believe I did. But what I remember most about that occasion was how much I struggled to hold back my own grief during the funeral service. I, too, was traumatised. I was a young father, twenty-seven years old. So for me, after that funeral service, the world of grieving was round the back of the crematorium chapel, out of sight, in floods of tears, before I rejoined the parents and other members of the family to shake hands with the mourners as they left the service. I'd done what was necessary and important for them, and then allowed myself to move from one world to the other. I didn't do it because the books or theories said I should. It was an intuitive thing.

But when I'd done with my immediate need to cry, it would have been wrong to remain in that world of grief when it wasn't appropriate or possible and expect everyone else to be there with me on my terms. Equally, it wasn't possible to live all the time in the world of coping and to pretend to myself that everything was OK. That's just not real. It's fine for the photo, but not for always.

A woman I worked with whose husband had died after fifty-two years of marriage once said to me, 'There are two things that have become more important to me than everything else in my bereavement …' To be honest, I was expecting something like, 'my Bible', or 'the family', or 'my best friend'. So, I was somewhat taken aback when she said: 'The first important thing for me is the ladies' toilet, where I can escape from a crowd, or even leave the family for a while, when things are getting too much, and I can really be myself for a few moments before I get back to "functioning".' I smiled when she added, 'I've still to come across anyone who questions whether I have a weak bladder!'

'And the second thing?' I asked.

'Oh,' she replied, 'that's my make-up bag. How absolutely essential has *that* become? Thank God for waterproof mascara!'

I have my equivalents to the ladies' as I slip into grief when I need to. I don't have a make-up bag, but I know that in different ways I can turn my white sweater around so that I can wear it back-to-front when necessary, and still look good for the photograph.

My father's tar stains on his white sweater were hidden from sight because they needed to be, and that was fine for the photograph. My father was able to tell the story of what was *really* happening because, at the right time, he needed to do that too. So I now have the complete picture – the one in the photograph, and the one of a child who got messed up when he shouldn't have done. It's good that there's more to my father than the well-behaved, respectable little boy in the family photo, don't you think?

Pictures

Picture this …
It's me, looking good.
'I'm fine, thank you; not too bad.
Yes, I'm getting there.'
It's me, looking quite good
for you.

Picture this …
All front, just for you.
'Quite well, thank you, as you can see;

mostly getting on.'
It's me, trying to be OK …
for now.

Picture this …
It's me, teary-eyed.
I *know* it's awful. But I smile,
keeping some control …
It's me, hiding the hellishness,
from you.

Picture this …
the mess, out of sight.
'It's been a bad day; lots of tears,
way out of control.'
It's me, just hanging on again,
for now.

Picture this …
It's me, turned out well.
'All sorted, thank you. Happy now?
I'm getting through.'
It's me, putting it on once more
for you.

Picture this …
The truth's well-concealed.
'No *way* can I let my mask slip!'
My grief is private.
It's me, good enough for photographs –
for now.

Chapter 4

Too many giants

The phrase 'tilting at windmills' has always intrigued me. It means, of course, that someone is attacking imaginary enemies, tackling something that's in the mind rather than reality, and having very little chance of success. But I have come to think of it in a different way when I work with bereaved people.

The expression comes from the novel *Don Quixote* by Miguel de Cervantes. To tilt is to joust – usually with a long lance – and to attack your enemy with speed and force. Cervantes has Don Quixote fighting windmills which he imagines are giants. A conversation between Don Quixote and his sidekick, Sancho Panza, gives us the context:

> *Just then they came in sight of thirty or forty windmills that rise from that plain. And no sooner did Don Quixote see them than he said to his squire, 'Fortune is guiding our affairs better than we ourselves could have wished. Do you see over yonder, friend Sancho, thirty or forty hulking giants? I intend to do battle with them and slay them. With their spoils we shall begin to be rich, for this is a righteous war and the removal of so foul a brood from off the face of the earth is a service God will bless.'*
>
> *'What giants?' asked Sancho Panza.*
>
> *'Those you see over there,' replied his master, 'with their long*

arms. Some of them have arms well nigh two leagues in length.'
'Take care, sir,' cried Sancho. 'Those over there are not giants
but windmills. Those things that seem to be their arms are sails
which, when they are whirled around by the wind, turn the
millstone.'

Don Quixote seeks to embark on a righteous war against what he
sees as giants, with his friend, Sancho Panza, seeking to pull him
back to reality by pointing out that they are nothing more or less
than windmills, with great sails whirling round in the wind.

It's a wonderful image, and it's not surprising that the popu-
larity of de Cervantes' novel caused the concept to slip into our
consciousness, so that today 'tilting at windmills' is used to
describe a confrontation or course of action where adversaries or
circumstances are incorrectly perceived.

In bereavement, people certainly have giants to fight. But it isn't
that the windmills are *false* giants and that the tilting has an unjus-
tified or misguided purpose. Rather, what were achievable goals
or targets when life was good and reasonably predictable have
become almost too gigantic to tackle while the grief of loss destabilises us or weighs us down. The simplest of tasks often
becomes burdensome. What in the past was easy or routine becomes
a giant that is difficult, or sometimes impossible, to face, far less
defeat. For people struggling to live with bereavement, it's not that
the windmills *look* like giants as they did for Don Quixote. It's that
the windmills *are* giants, frightening in their magnitude.

Those struggling with bereavement are drawn, like Don
Quixote, into their own 'righteous war' – or at least that's how it
seems – attacked on all sides by a 'foul brood' of issues which are
hard to bear. From changing a light bulb to sleeping alone; from
writing Christmas cards to choosing wallpaper; from buying a
plane ticket to mowing the lawn; from dealing with HMRC to

renewing the car insurance; from attending a concert to disposing of clothes. It can often feel that there are too many frightening giants to be faced.

James was a middle-aged man whose father had died. It wasn't a traumatic death. Indeed, the passing of the eighty-seven-year-old man was, in many ways, a relief to James and his siblings. Their father had been frail for many years, suffering the debilitating effects of bronchitis and COPD, the inevitable results of many years as a heavy smoker. The 'package of care' which allowed him to remain at home continued to increase till it had reached its maximum. Long-term care in a local nursing home was the next thing that would have to be considered. But James and his family were spared that set of decisions when the old man slipped away quietly in his sleep.

The effects on James of his father's death were worse than he expected, although his two sisters appeared to be coping better than he was. He felt exhausted most of the time, his concentration levels had taken a dip and he wasn't sleeping well. He was constantly irritable, and his motivation to act and make decisions was at the lowest point that he could remember.

Standing back from the situation, it would have been easy enough to figure out why: the loss of the second parent; the 'orphan' issue (albeit James was fifty-one); the fact that he was the only son, and the importance of the close bond he'd had with his father; the 'male' issue, something in him, or in the expectations of others, that said he should be staying strong to be the necessary support for his wife, sisters and children; the 'tidying-up-of-affairs' that had to be seen to, dealing with HMRC, lawyers, insurance companies, pensions, and much more; the guilt, irrational though he knew it to be, around 'Could I have done more?', or 'Did I wish him away in the end?'

But James couldn't stand back from things. He wasn't a Sancho

Panza, watching it all from the sidelines, able to make comments and offer advice. He was right in the middle of it. He was a veritable Don Quixote, with an army of giants to face, and the giants were getting bigger, and more threatening … and James was beginning to panic.

It all came to a head in his half-year appraisal with his head of department at work. James was a history teacher – and a good one too, by all accounts. He was well used to 'performance appraisals', and they hadn't been a problem for him in the past. This one wasn't the crucial annual assessment. It was a 'touch base', a helpful mid-year review. It was – or it should have been – routine. But on this occasion the Head of History wasn't happy, and James knew why. Things were being missed. James had lost his sparkle. Other people were feeling they were 'carrying him' a bit. In the days and weeks immediately after his father's death, everyone in the department – and, indeed, in the whole staffroom – had been supportive, understanding, patient, accommodating. But now, five months on? Could he expect such tolerance to continue? And wasn't he letting down the students?

It was a wake-up call for James. To start with, he had to recognise that the lethargy and loss of drive were normal. Then he had to work out what was happening by taking a long, hard look at things; checking out with others why and how they were going through similar experiences; putting some strategies in place … All of this was the beginning of a series of improvements for James. In time, he got over the period of panic. In many ways, he knew that the hard work had just begun, but at least he had come to understand what was happening to him and had started to deal with it in a more positive fashion.

For James, his windmills in bereavement were giants which, in the past, he could tackle and defeat with ease. But in the aftermath of the loss of his father they had become an overwhelming army that had almost brought him to his knees.

It happens for everyone in bereavement in one way or another. Sometimes it's the small things that turn into scary giants. In one of our bereavement groups, we got on to the subject of 'doing things for the first time', and several 'tilting at windmills' issues. Ellen, a widow in her late sixties, a slight and somewhat shy soul, had been quite quiet as the discussion moved this way and that. But, in her own time, she chipped in with her own contribution to the conversation.

She explained that her 'tilting at windmills' event had been dealing with her husband's clothes which had been left largely untouched for some months after the funeral. In time, she decided it was necessary to 'get on with it'. She'd managed to do just that, she explained, even though it had been very hard indeed. She'd decided she needed to do it 'in a one-er' – when her energy levels had improved sufficiently, and her motivation had returned – and not in bits and pieces. It had taken her a whole weekend. When she was finished, there were a dozen black bin bags and several cardboard boxes scattered around the bedroom, the living-room and the hallway, carefully sorted and labelled: 'Family', 'Charity Shop' and 'Rubbish'.

The bags of rubbish were dumped in the council wheelie-bin outside her flat. The 'family' bags and boxes were moved into the spare bedroom for her daughters to look through later. And that left six bags and three boxes for the charity shop.

Because she didn't drive, Ellen had phoned the charity shop first thing on the Monday morning, and an arrangement was made for the boxes and bags to be collected at two o'clock on the following Tuesday afternoon. That night, Ellen had the best sleep she'd had in ages. The following day, she waited for two o'clock to come around when everything would be collected. But the promised time came and went, and no one appeared from the charity shop. Three o'clock passed. Ellen could feel herself getting tense. Her head started to pound. 'Was it no' hard enough to get it sorted, and now they're no' comin' to take it away,' she'd said out loud in her exasperation.

We'd all been listening with rapt attention as Ellen's story unfolded. There had been many nods of recognition and understanding. But then this frail, elderly lady offered us an amazing revelation that left us shocked, then amused, then full of admiration. I'll let Ellen speak for herself …

'See … Ah could feel masel' gettin' angrier an' angrier. My mutterin' tae masel' turned intae swearin' … an' that's no' like me at a'. Ah kent ah should hae phoned the charity shop tae ask whit wis happenin', but ah wis beyond thinkin' straight. Ah wis seethin'. An' when four o'clock wis announced by the chimes o' the mantle-clock in the livin' room, ah just lost it! An' ah jist let go with a blood-curdlin' scream the likes o' which had niver came oot' o' ma mooth afore. Ah jist screamed, an' screamed, an' screamed. An' when the bliddy clock chimed the quarter hour, ah took the damn thing aff the mantle an' smashed it wi' a' ma might aff the living' room wa'!'

There were gasps of disbelief round the table, and Ellen was crying now. But there was no embarrassment and no apology. Instead what we saw in her was relief that people could listen to her story and not judge her harshly. And what I saw from the others in the group were faces changing from shock to admiration. Here were no Sancho Panzas, saying – or even thinking – 'I think you might have got it all wrong!' Instead, here were people who knew what this felt like. Though they may not ever have done what Ellen had done, they knew well enough the battles with windmills in their own lives.

Ellen caught the mood, and, wiping her eyes with a tissue, she said, 'An' the funny thing was, just then the doorbell rang. It was the man frae the charity shop. "Sorry I'm late, missus," he said. "Van problems. Is this the stuff?" sez he, looking round the hall an' clockin' the boxes an' bags o' clothes. "Leave it tae' me, hen, and I'll get it sorted." But ah wis glad he didnae see the smashed clock, eh? Maybe he wid hae thought ah wis nuts!"

There was a burst of laughter followed by lots of positive comments. 'I don't think you're nuts,' one of the other ladies said. 'I think you've done good. You're a feisty woman, that's for sure. Well done you.' And I'll never forget the vigorous nod of Ellen's head and the sense of satisfaction and achievement it showed.

In bereavement, especially in the initial stages, the ability to concentrate and make reasonable and rational decisions is often severely compromised. There is often a loss of motivation, an inability to think clearly, an avoidance of decision-making because there is just too much pressure, and so on. Not surprisingly, this can lead to a loss of confidence – such as James had experienced at work – and the fear that you might never regain the ability to think clearly and rationally and be on top of all the decision-making which had been integral to your daily living and needed to be again. It's hard when the giants are winning. It can also create pressure – as Ellen found – when things don't work out the way you hope or expect, pressure that can burst out in frustration, temper and aggression – and smashing clocks! – when no matter how you try, you're on the losing side of the 'righteous' battle. There are always windmills to be tilted at, tasks to complete, decisions to make, plans to formulate, projects to finish. And when there isn't the energy or clarity, and when attempts end in failure or abandonment of a process, people often feel things are getting worse rather than better – which I'm sure Ellen might have been told if she'd shared her story with any Sancho Panzas in her family or among her circle of friends.

The bottom line is this ... bereaved people need reassurance that their capacity to think clearly and make positive decisions has not departed them completely. It has just been placed temporarily on hold. It has been compromised by the enormity of the loss and its emotional implications. But it has not gone for ever.

The corollary is that those who are bereaved need to be encouraged to give themselves credit when they do things well, when a decision *is* made, when a plan has been achieved or when a process of working things out *has* been successful. And if they are unable to give *themselves* credit, all the more reason why they need to hear a 'well done' from others and be given affirmation for winning a small battle – achieving something they never thought they would ever be able to sort out.

Was it right to offer a 'well done' to Ellen when she'd expressed her feelings by dramatically smashing her clock? I genuinely think it was.

Caroline was wrestling with the same issues as Ellen and James, but in a very different way. She had her own giants to face. She was a bright and lively woman, whose husband, Barry, had died tragically before he'd reached forty. They'd had no children, and now Caroline, widowed in her mid-thirties, was trying to face the future without her 'rock and mainstay'. She held down a responsible job in management in a big insurance company. But she had hit a major stumbling block – a big windmill to tilt at, it appeared. She had no idea what she was going to do with her husband's ashes.

Barry had chosen to be cremated. Caroline had no problem with that. But she wasn't expecting the funeral director's question.

'Would you prefer your husband's ashes to be retained or dispersed in the crematorium's Garden of Remembrance, Mrs Fisher?' had been the dignified enquiry.

What? WHAT? had been the reply screaming in her head. *Barry never gave me instructions about that!* But after the initial panic, she'd agreed that the ashes should 'be retained'. She doesn't know why she chose that, because she had no idea what she was going to do with the ashes. There were too many other things to think about, affairs to be put in order, bills to pay, decisions to make, work to get back to. There was an army of windmills to be faced. Decisions about the ashes could wait.

And wait is what the ashes had to do – at the beginning in the undertaker's office and more recently in the bottom of the wardrobe in Caroline's spare room. And that's where they still lay, in a plastic urn with a 'Barry Fisher' label taped to the side, inside a velvet bag, closed tight with a plaited drawstring, inside a Co-op polybag, inside a black bin liner, inside an old rucksack.

One evening, midway through a discussion with other bereaved relatives, and while we were exploring motivation and decision-making issues, Caroline told us she'd made up her mind about the ashes. She was going to scatter them during the holiday weekend that was coming up, and she'd tell us all about it when she came back the next week. So, as soon as we'd sat down the following Wednesday, the opening question was, 'Well, how did you get on with the ashes?'

She'd taken the ashes to the Forest of Dean, she told us, a part of the country she and Barry had enjoyed over the years. She'd booked into a guest house they'd used several times. Though the folk there knew about Barry's death, Caroline didn't tell them about the ashes. That was too private. On the Saturday afternoon, the ashes had been scattered as per her plan, and Caroline shared with us the mixture of emotion and relief she'd experienced. Everything had worked out well and she was left with a sense of closure.

Those in the group listened intently to her story. There were comments of admiration, empathy and genuine support from everyone. But, towards the end of the session, Caroline indicated there was a part of the story she hadn't told us yet. When she'd been packing the car in Edinburgh ready for her trip south, she'd opened the boot and thrown her case in, followed by the old rucksack with the ashes inside. But as she was sitting in the car ready for the off, she thought, *I can't have Barry travelling all the way to the Forest of Dean in the boot of the car. He'll not like it in there.* 'I know it's silly,' she told us, 'but I just couldn't just leave him in the boot. So I took him in the old rucksack and put him in the passenger seat beside me. And then I thought, *He'll not be safe if he doesn't have a seat-belt on.* So there I was, travelling down the motorway, with Barry strapped in, safe in the seat beside me all the way.'

We laughed at the picture – and the honesty – of it all. 'But that's not all,' Caroline continued. 'I pulled into a service-station for a coffee halfway there, and I was walking into the cafe when I had another thought: *What if the car gets nicked? Barry'll be gone, stolen, off, and I'll not know where he is.* So, I went back to the car and rescued him. He sat beside me in the cafe. I had a coffee and a bun, and I almost bought a tea and a chocolate biscuit for him too. And I wondered what people going past would have thought if they knew there was a mad woman in a motorway cafe with her husband in a purple velvet bag, closed tight with a plaited drawstring, inside a Co-op polybag, inside a black bin liner, inside an old rucksack, sitting at her feet.'

They *might* have said something if they'd been Sancho Panza and she'd been Don Quixote. But Caroline had no need of a comment or a judgement from a sidekick or from anyone else. She had tackled her big giant – and other little ones she'd had to face up to along the way – and had come out victorious. No windmill waving its gigantic arms was going to defeat the likes of Caroline Fisher. And I'm sure that if James and Ellen had been listening to Caroline's story with the rest of us, they would have wholeheartedly agreed!

Stuff

'So, what will you do with the stuff,' they said,
'what'll you do with the stuff?
We know that you're finding it rough,' they said,
'and our pleadings you'll try to rebuff.
You've put it off quite long enough,' they said.
'You'll have to start acting real tough,
and stop yourself having a huff,' they said.
'So, what will you do with the stuff?'

   'I'll deal with the stuff when I can,' I said,
   'I'll face up to things when I can.
   Please, let me be just as I am,' I said,
   'And stop saying, "It's time you began …"
   Don't force me to be superman,' I said.
   'I'll make it a part of my plan,
   when I'm a more organised man,' I said.
   'I'll sort through the stuff when I can.'

'But, when will you sort out the things,' they said,
'oh, when will you tackle the things?
The dresses, the shoes, and the rings,' they said,
'no matter what pain it still brings?
We know that your sorrow still stings,' they said,
'but you can't hide away in the wings.
Come on! You should give it a fling,' they said.
'So, what will you do with those things?'

   'I'll deal with the things in a while,' I said.
   The things can just wait for a while.
   For now, it's too much of a trial,' I said.
   'I can't even manage a smile.

Despite your persuasion and guile,' I said,
'which I know now is always your style …
you know, it's beginning to rile,' I said,
'I'll get to those things in a while.'

'But what will you do with all this?' they said.
'Just what'll you do with all this?'
'We think that there's something amiss,' they said.
'The truth is too real to dismiss.
We know that your life is the pits,' they said,
'without any glamour or glitz.
But nobody promised you bliss,' they said.
'So, what will you do with all this?'

'All this can just wait, can't you see?' I said.
'Though clearly you'll never agree!
The advice you still offer for free,' I said,
'your "shoulds" and your "musts" and your "please",
put far too much pressure on me,' I said.
'Just give me some space to be free
to work out what I need to be,' I said.
'Be patient and wait till I'm me.'

Chapter 5

As others see us

The poem 'To a Louse' was written by Robert Burns on the occasion of 'seeing one on a Lady's Bonnet at Church'. Burns was a keen observer and interpreter of life in all its forms – from toothache to dogs, from haggis to the affairs of a nation, from the welfare of a mouse to the effects of the demon drink, from the emotions of love to the state of the Church.

Robert Burns, like many of his contemporaries, had what could be described as a 'love–hate' relationship with the Presbyterian Church of 18th-century Scotland. He attended worship, as did many of his peers, but was also regularly faced with the discipline of the Church for the waywardness of his morals, and he was called to account for his misdemeanours several times. But above all, Burns detested what he saw as the cant and hypocrisy of the Church, its hierarchy and injustice, and the better-than-thou attitude he saw in many of those who were supposedly 'the pillars of the Kirk'.

Not surprisingly, during the interminably long sermons which would have been commonplace in Burns' day, his mind would be inclined to wander, and the creative musings of this remarkable poet would find plenty of scope for development. So, in the paradox of seeing a 'wee beastie' crawling on the fine hat of a churchgoing lady, Burns takes time to reflect on the welfare and circumstances of the louse and, in so doing, gives thought to the issues of his own life and that of all humanity.

Perhaps he scribbled the beginning of his poem in the flyleaf of his Bible or Psalter – who knows? (just as I have done often enough myself when I don't want to lose the thread of a thought or the beginning of a concept). But even if he didn't, we're all the better for Burns reflecting on the moment and writing such remarkable verses thereafter.

Here's the poem. I make no apology for offering it in the Broad Scots of Burns' own culture, but I promise I'll help you with the final verse.

Ha! whaur ye gaun, ye crowlin ferlie?
Your impudence protects you sairly;
I canna say but ye strunt rarely,
Owre gauze and lace;
Tho', faith! I fear ye dine but sparely
On sic a place.

Ye ugly, creepin, blastit wonner,
Detested, shunn'd by saunt an' sinner,
How daur ye set your fit upon her –
Sae fine a lady?
Gae somewhere else and seek your dinner
On some poor body.

Swith! in some beggar's haffet squattle;
There ye may creep, and sprawl, and sprattle,
Wi' ither kindred, jumping cattle,
In shoals and nations;
Whaur horn nor bane ne'er daur unsettle
Your thick plantations.

Now haud you there, ye're out o' sight,
Below the fatt'rels, snug and tight;
Na, faith ye yet! ye'll no be right,

Till ye've got on it –
The verra tapmost, tow'rin height
O' Miss' bonnet.

My sooth! right bauld ye set your nose out,
As plump an' grey as ony groset:
O for some rank, mercurial rozet,
Or fell, red smeddum,
I'd gie you sic a hearty dose o't,
Wad dress your droddum.

I wad na been surpris'd to spy
You on an auld wife's flainen toy;
Or aiblins some bit dubbie boy,
On's wyliecoat;
But Miss' fine Lunardi! fye!
How daur ye do't?

O Jeany, dinna toss your head,
An' set your beauties a' abread!
Ye little ken what cursed speed
The blastie's makin:
Thae winks an' finger-ends, I dread,
Are notice takin.

O wad some Power the giftie gie us
To see oursels as ithers see us!
It wad frae mony a blunder free us,
An' foolish notion:
What airs in dress an' gait wad lea'e us,
An' ev'n devotion!

It's the final stanza that is the 'punchline' of the poem, and one which I find, again and again, is apposite to the bereavement work with which I am involved. Let me explain – and begin with what for some might be a necessary translation ...

Burns wishes we had some power, a gift of interpretation or understanding, that would allow us to see and know ourselves as others do. And if that gift were available to us, what disasters might be avoided, and unfortunate ideas abandoned, to allow us to escape the consequences of our own mistakes?

Perhaps, then, with the knowledge of ourselves that others may already have of us, we might not show we are the 'airs in dress' as we are often inclined to do. Might we come to know that the airs and graces of presentation, attitude and even holiness that we continue to show to the world can be dispensed with? If only *we* could see through the 'act' we put on and get to the truth of who we are – as others are able to do more readily – the better we might be.

None of us wears our heart on our sleeve all the time – or even most of the time – in our daily living. We wear the masks, the *personae,* of the parts we wish to play and the attitudes we wish to convey. It's a rare, bold and confident person who will 'let it all hang out' and who doesn't give a hoot how this will look to others. We live with masks all the time – from the fine bonnet in church, to the hypocrisy of a 'holier-than-thou' approach to life.

This concept of 'mask-wearing' is seldom more obvious than in bereavement. It goes back to 'wearing the tar-stained sweater back-to-front' as we explored earlier.

'How are you?' 'I'm fine.' And the coping mask stays firmly in place.

'Doing OK?' 'Not too bad.' And the positive persona is offered as reassurance.

'Good to see you again.' 'Yes, good to be back.' And we have successfully hidden reality.

We do this for valid reasons, of course. We've all done it for ourselves and with others. But sometimes – for everyone's benefit

– the mask needs to be challenged.

Of course, that often means we have to be honest about how *bad* things are. And we need people to listen and to allow us to be truly ourselves – as we have explored earlier too. But I've become convinced that we also need affirmation and a sensitive directness in bereavement. We need people who, in honesty and love, can tell us what we often can't see for ourselves about how we have progressed. Not platitudes, not flannel, not telling people what they need to hear and so reinforcing their mask-wearing. But being encouraging in their honesty and open in their affirmation.

In our monthly hospice bereavement support groups we had a woman, Gwen, who was too emotional to speak during her first meeting. It had only been three months since her husband, Hector, had died. He was eighty-seven and they'd been married for sixty-two years. Gwen's grief was still so raw that it was too much for her to talk about. She cried on and off for the hour or so we were together. I didn't think she'd come back the following month, because quite clearly the pain of her loss was close to overwhelming her.

But she did come back, this time with a shopping bag. Once again, she couldn't say much, but during the discussion she asked if she could show us what she'd brought with her and, just before our group session came to an end, she unearthed from her bag her wedding photograph, along with a picture of herself in her teenage years when she and Hector had first met, and one of a singularly handsome young man in Air Force uniform. There were tears from Gwen, and genuine interest from the others. It was a lovely moment.

Gwen attended the groups every month for another seven months or so, and little by little she was able to talk and share more and more as time went by. The month before the anniversary of Hector's death she launched with some vehemence into a story about the Gas Board, and delays, and workmen, and phone calls, and anger ... nothing short of a rant! 'I'm not coping any better than I was before,' she said. 'I'm all over the place.' (Clearly, the Gas Board windmill was a giant that was almost impossible to defeat!) She broke down in tears.

I was about to offer her some words of sympathy and consolation, when one of the other women in the group got in first. 'Do you remember what you were like when you first came here?' The silence of the group allowed her to go further. 'You couldn't speak, woman, you were so broken. And then you brought yon photos along. Lovely, it was. D'you remember?' Gwen nodded slowly. 'Well! There you are! And look at you now! Feisty, articulate, angry, animated, motivated, up-for-the-fight ... So if that's not progress in this past year, I don't know what is ...' And Gwen nodded – and smiled through her tears. Another person could see what she couldn't see for herself – and had been prepared to say so in the right way and at the right time.

To see ourselves as others see us ... Too close to it? Progress is hard to see, or understand, or believe. But with a trusting 'outside view', offered in wisdom, and honesty, and love, a new world of understanding and acceptance can open up.

When Rodney attended a bereavement support programme, he was clearly struggling to make sense of life without the wife who had been his companion and mainstay for forty-eight years. Rodney's happy marriage had been one of those relationships where divisions of responsibility between husband and wife had been established early on and hadn't changed much in all the years they'd been together. In short ... he earned the money, and Greta did pretty well everything else. She was the planner, the shopper, the cook, the cleaner, the organiser, the homemaker, and ... Well, I think you get the picture.

It may seem odd to those of us who have a different balance of responsibilities in our marriages, but for Rodney and Greta it worked perfectly well. There was no malice or exploitation in it. Their relationship was loving, their roles and responsibilities clear and unchanging and their marriage perfectly happy. Until, that is, Greta died. It was a relatively quick death, and a few months after Greta's cancer diagnosis Rodney was bereft of his lifelong companion and the love of his life. Conversations with him in the early weeks and months of his loss were heart-rending. Life on his own made no sense, he said. Continuing with daily life without Greta had little point. He'd lost everything. He described it as 'half of me being torn away'.

I touched base with Rodney a couple of times during the first two or three months of his bereavement. He wanted me to fix things, to make it better, to take the pain away. Of course, I could do none of these things, and I know Rodney felt I'd failed him and, to be honest, there was a bit of me that felt I was failing too. What was to be done with this broken, devastated, hurting man? I was relieved when I heard that Rodney had decided to join one of our Acorns programmes. This particular programme was being held in the community room of a local library and was attended by eight or ten other bereaved people. Most of them had lost a life partner, and several of them were around the same age as Rodney. There were a couple of folk who were recently bereaved of a parent too. Rodney was the only man in the group.

The first meeting of a support programme is always the most raw, often with the shedding of many tears. Not surprisingly, it was extremely emotional for Rodney as he shared the depth of his sorrow and his struggles to make sense of living without Greta. I remember he talked a lot, not so that he dominated the group, but just because a lot of things tumbled out at once. But people were patient with him and sympathetic, as indeed everyone was with everyone else. I considered it to be a successful opening to the programme.

It didn't feel that way for Rodney, though. It was clearly hard for him, and he whispered in my ear as he rushed away at the end of that first session that he might not come back to continue with the programme. But to my surprise – and, it appeared, to everyone else's too – he did come back the following week. He wasn't quite so tearful this time, but his communication of his issues was as heart-rending as ever. And over the weeks we learned of his struggles with cooking, going to bed alone, working the washing machine. But we were also encouraged to hear of the other love of his life in competition with Greta – playing the drums in a local Scottish country dance band.

He'd been in the band over many years, and had played with them at weddings, ceilidhs and functions most weekends. But his enthusiasm for it all had gone, and he couldn't summon up any motivation to get back to the band. 'What right do I have to enjoy myself,' he had said through more tears, 'when my wife is dead?'

We were on week five of the six-week programme, and within the established trust and openness of a group of people who'd come to know, understand and support each other over the weeks the sharing had reached quite a deep level. Rodney was on one of his rants (as one woman had described it – caringly – the previous week) about his struggles with daily living, when the same woman – herself widowed after more than forty years of marriage – blurted out in her exasperation, 'Oh for goodness' sake, man. Just look at your shirt!' It took us all by surprise, and we all turned to look at Rodney. I was expecting to see a soup stain down his front, or a grubby collar, or frayed cuffs. He'd been stopped in his tracks too and, as surprised as we were, gasped – somewhat angrily – 'What do you mean? What's wrong with my shirt?'

'Nothing wrong at all,' the woman responded. 'I was just thinking how smart you were looking. Look at the sleeves of your shirt? You've got creases down them sharp enough to prune roses.

Who did that?'

'I did?' Rodney responded, sheepishly. 'I did an ironing this morning.'

'There you are!' the woman responded, with a note of triumph in her voice. 'There you are. *You* did that. *You* ironed your own shirt – and better than I ever could. *You're* the one looking after yourself. *You're* the one beginning to make sense of being on your own, keeping your standards up, presenting yourself well. *You*! Well done, man. From where I'm sitting, you're doing a damn good job. And I hope you play the drums in your band half as well as you can iron a shirt.' There was a spontaneous – though gentle – round of applause, and many nods and comments thereafter to reinforce this forceful rebuke. And as I looked up from the sharp creases on the sleeves of Rodney's shirt to see how he was responding to all of this, I found the biggest smile I had seen on his flushed, embarrassed face.

Someone had seen from the outside what Rodney, immersed in his grief, couldn't or wouldn't see for himself. And in the trust, openness, honesty and care of a group of fellow travellers he'd heard an affirmation that was clearly important to him. It's not too much to say that what became known that week, and in the final session of our programme a week later, as the 'sharp-creases-in-the-shirt-sleeves' comment was a turning point for Rodney in his journey of loss.

How do I know that? We don't offer follow-up in our support programmes, though there are times when people return to another programme some months or, indeed, years down the line of their bereavement journey. So, most of the time, we have no knowledge of how people are coping and what part our support groups have played in their ongoing welfare. Not so with Rodney …

I was at a St Andrew's Night ceilidh in a neighbouring village a year or so later when I realised it was the self-same Rodney who was sitting behind the drums in the band. He was – as we say in Scotland – 'giving it laldy', beating time with impeccable rhythm, and clearly enjoying himself. He spotted me when I was whirling round the dance floor during a *Gay Gordons* and, with a big smile and a crash on his cymbal, acknowledged my presence as I did his. We had a chat over a cup of tea during the interval. He was in great form, and I was delighted to see when he returned to his place behind his drum-kit, that he still had incredibly sharp creases in the sleeves of his white shirt.

Back to the ceilidh band for Rodney, it appeared. But it was clearly more than that. For it was back to living, back to motivation, back to making sense of a world without Greta. And I couldn't help thinking that the 'sharp-creases-in-the-shirt-sleeves' comment may have been the beginning of all of that.

Some of the people who benefit most from the bereavement groups in which I've been involved over the years are those who have had to 'wear masks', to take on this *persona* or that in order to portray to others what they feel they should be portraying. The reasons for this could be the subject of another whole book. But we know it's happening to others because we know we do it ourselves. Often it's necessary – for family, employment, or social reasons. Sometimes it's through fear of finding something in yourself you can't or won't acknowledge. Occasionally the reasons for it are quite beyond our control. But if it happens, and if we know it happens, and if we're aware of it because we see it in ourselves, all the more reason to accept it for what it is – a legitimate coping strategy – and also to place alongside it opportunities to take the masks off or to adjust the *persona* in a trusting, open, non-judgemental environment.

So let the final word in this chapter be Celeste's. She was a widow in her late seventies who joined one of our bereavement programmes around nine months after the death of Bennet, her husband of fifty-five years. Bennet had been a high-ranking police officer who, in retirement, had founded and run an apparently successful private security company. Life had been good for them both, and their family and social life had been full and fulfilling. Bennet's funeral was bigger than Celeste could ever have imagined, and that was the beginning of her 'coping persona', as she called it. Dignified, strong, vivacious, refined, and all that was expected of her in respectable Edinburgh society, Celeste coped – and showed the world how she coped – as she, and others, expected her to do.

But in bereavement, Celeste's world began to fall apart. Losing her life-partner was bad enough, but being the grieving widow in what she called a 'couple society' hit her hard. She reckoned she could have expected and coped with that, if that had been all. But it wasn't. For as Bennet's 'estate' was being dealt with, debts were uncovered, small at the start, and then bigger and more extensive. Celeste never revealed the extent of the problem. It was enough for us to know that alongside the death of her husband and her continued acceptance in 'society', she was also now having to cope with the death of the *image* of her husband, which all too quickly was being replaced by one of deceit, lies and cheating. So Celeste's issue was this – and I'll let her speak for herself …

'I am what I need to be with the people who need me to be that person. I'm not going to lose face alongside all the other things I've lost. I cannot, and I will not, wear my heart on my sleeve. It's just not me. So no one else knows what I'm living with now. But I need somewhere – and you're the ones who're going to get it all – where I can let my mask slip and tell it as it is. I need people who don't really know me – and who're not bothered about my image – to accept me as I am. And who am I? I'm the dignified, refined Edinburgh lady who is now ferociously angry with her dead husband.'

Her final phrase showed us all she was wearing no masks for us. She didn't need to hide behind any persona. She had found a place to 'tell it as it is' and received no judgement or condemnation in response. How do I know that? Not just because that's what Celeste told us herself but because one of the other women in the group – who came from what can only be described as a different stratum of society than Celeste's – put a hand on hers and whispered, 'Just you be angry, hen. If it was me, I'd be usin' a few sweary-words too, and be leavin' him without a name!'

'To see ourselves as others see us …': the process of beginning to remove our masks and to find acceptance and understanding – even across social divides – from people whose experience resonates with our own.

'To see ourselves as others see us …': the process of beginning to live again began with an affirmation of one widowed man's ability to learn how to iron his shirts, and the willingness of one observant woman who, like Robert Burns, saw what she saw, and was prepared to offer the affirmation and reassurance that a grieving man couldn't, or wouldn't, see for himself.

To see myself

To see myself as you would see me? There's a thing to do.
To know myself as you might know me? There's a thing that's new.
To find myself as you would find me? What a thing to learn!
Who am I to those around me? So much to discern …

To see myself reflected in another's views, is good.
With insights, well directed, I can feel I'm understood.
I'll benefit from what's been seen and not be too disturbed.
To see myself as others see me – that's not so absurd!

So, come to me with honesty, and gently help me out.
There's no need to be forceful; you don't have to scream or shout!
Accept me as you find me; that's my simple, heartfelt plea.
To see myself as others do – now, that's the task for me!

Mon	Tue	Wed	Thu	Fri	Sat	Sun
			1	2	3	4
5	6	7	8	9	10	11
12	13	14	15	16	17	18
19	20	21	22	23	24	25
26	27	28	29	30		

Chapter 6

How long?

It would be great if the processes of grief and loss could be measured, quantified and compared with the experiences of others. But measuring grief isn't like recording the distance of a discus-throw or the length of a hall carpet. Nor is it possible to break down the grief journey and manage it like the stages tackled by a team in a marathon. There is no rulebook or measuring-stick for bereavement.

When the Swiss/American psychiatrist Elisabeth Kübler-Ross wrote in 1969 about bereavement issues, she informed us that people's reactions to bereavement should be accepted as normal. When she published *On death and dying*[3] and postulated for the first time 'the Kübler-Ross model' (more popularly known as 'the five stages of grief'), a series of emotions experienced by terminally ill patients or those who are bereaved – denial, anger, bargaining, depression and acceptance – it was a revelation. Not surprisingly, this model was quickly accepted by both the general public and medical professionals. But this acceptance also caused problems, for it created a presumption that there is always a rigid structure to grief with distinct and measurable stages.

The processes of loss can be understood to follow a 'healing' progression, just as bowel surgery, a broken leg or radiotherapy result in a pattern of healing and restoration to health. But a linear approach in bereavement is not consistently supported by the majority of current research. Indeed, it is interesting to note that in later life Kübler-Ross herself suggested that the stages are *not* a linear and predictable progression, and that she regretted writing about them in a way that was misunderstood. Rather, they are a collation of experiences common to bereaved people that can occur in any order – if at all.

In recent years, grief theories have become more flexible, reflecting a deeper understanding of the reality of the experience of loss. Here are a few current examples:

John Bowlby's 'Attachment Theory' (1969, 1973), as the title suggests, is related to an understanding of the childhood attachments which are created with key people, primarily parents, in our early years of development. Whether these attachments are good or bad, understood or seldom reflected on, there is a clear correlation between them and the way we process any bereavement, when the physical relationship with a person is no longer available to us.

In the 1990s, Colin Murray Parkes wrote about 'shifting pictures'[4], an understanding of how we cope over time, and seldom in the same way and at the same rate as other people. If a death has been a difficult one, for example, it's not surprising that the images that people are often stuck with for a long time are those around the events of the death.

William Worden's 1992 theory, defined as 'The tasks of mourning'[5], indicates that grieving is hard work. For everyone it's a struggle which drains them physically, mentally, emotionally and spiritually, and there is rarely a definitive pattern.

In 1996, Dennis Klass, Phyllis Silverman and Steven Nickman postulated a theory called 'Continuing Bonds'[6]. The shape of those bonds and the expression of them will be different for everyone, and will be reconstructed over varying lengths of time. We are all unique, and our relationships with those who have died will be different for each person.

More recently, as previously mentioned, Margaret Stroebe and

Henk Schut's 'Dual Process Model'[7] showed that in bereavement we begin to live in two worlds – the world of loss, and the world of coping; the world of grief, and the world of possibilities. We will swing from one to the other over time and the timescale involved is never definable.[8]

Gregor's wife, Rhoda, died seven years after she was first diagnosed with early-onset dementia. She was fifty-one when her life came to a tragic but predictable end. At the start of Rhoda's illness, Gregor knew it was going to be a long and difficult road, and as his wife declined further he gave himself totally and self-sacrificially to her care. Rhoda's personality, behaviour and mood were increasingly affected. But had they not promised each other 'in sickness and in health …'?

At first it was a juggling act of holding down his job while also being a carer. In time it was giving up work because the strain was too much. And, at the end, it was being a constant companion. There were times when Gregor was worn out and hated every minute of what he was going through. He told me several times during his wife's illness that he wished Rhoda would just go, for there was no quality of life for her – or for him – in these circumstances. I never disagreed. In time, I conducted Rhoda's funeral. Gregor confided in me that Rhoda had, in truth, 'died several years ago, but she only gave up her life a week past Tuesday.'

Gregor remarried six months after Rhoda's death. The news took everyone by surprise. He married one of his wife's carers, a woman he'd got to know and love over the long periods of time they had spent together during Rhoda's illness. I was pleased for them, and wrote to them to wish them well in their marriage. A new beginning, I thought, for two people with, hopefully, years of life ahead of them. However, that's not the way Gregor's two daughters saw it. They felt it was too early for their father to remarry. They accused him of disloyalty to their mother's memory.

They assured him they would have 'nothing to do with a bloody stepmother'. (Yes, that's *actually* what they said …)

Gregor was, of course, distraught, caught as he was between his love for his daughters and love for his new wife. 'They've got a timescale in their heads,' he said, 'a measurement, stages, appropriateness, when things are expected and accepted. That timescale began for them when Rhoda died. But not for me. I've been living with this for years, dealing with her death long before she died. That's why I need to do what's right for me now. It's my timescale, my journey, my measurement, and not anyone else's.'

It's years since I've been in touch with Gregor. I hope things worked out OK between him and his daughters. But I know he was right. There was no set pattern he could work to just because of what other people saw or expected.

The poet and prelate Richard Corbet, who was Chaplain to King James I at the beginning of the 17th century, wrote this to his son Vincent as he reflected on the value and worth of the young man's life:

> I wish thee all thy mother's graces,
> Thy father's fortunes, and his places.
> I wish thee friends, and one at court,
> Not to build on, but support,
> To keep thee, not in doing many
> Oppressions, but from suffering any.

A loving father, hoping his son would carry the influence of both his mother and his father with him through all his days.

In his book of spiritual reflections, *The Prophet,* the Lebanese writer Kahlil Gibran, offers this on the meaning of marriage:

> You were born together, and together you shall be forevermore.
> But let there be spaces in your togetherness,

And let the winds of the heavens dance between you.
Love one another, but make not a bond of love:
Give your hearts, but not into each other's keeping.
And stand together yet not too near together:
For the pillars of the temple stand apart,
And the oak tree and the cypress grow not in each other's shadow.

It is clear from both of these poetic reflections that, in seeking to live a full and productive life, we carry with us the depth and importance of loving relationships, of influence and nurture, through all our days. The ways we have loved and are loved, and the people with whom we have shared those loving bonds, are crucial to a life of fulfilment and well-being.

Is it any wonder, therefore, that in bereavement we yearn for the continuation of these bonds of love? For without them, and especially when bereft of their physical manifestation, we feel uncertain and alone, confused and cast adrift, unfulfilled and fearful. And is it any wonder that this yearning doesn't fit into a timescale or pattern that other people expect?

Give your hearts, but not into each other's keeping, Gibran suggests. And yet that's not always how people do things. *And stand together yet not too near together*, he tells us. But that's not always the way things work out with our partners, marriages, siblings, parents, children, friendships … So we grieve out of the depths of our relationships, and when we have given our hearts into each other's keeping, no matter what the relationship is, then the grief we experience in bereavement will be, and should be, extraordinarily painful.

Mike Wilson, a retired GP who is one of the resource people in our Acorns groups, describes the ongoing processes of bereavement as standing on the shore and watching the tide go out. It moves away, then it comes back, sometimes faster and further than you expect so that your feet get wet. Then it moves away again, further out, and you think it's gone and you're safe, because it's a little bit further away than it was before and no longer threatens you. And then a bigger wave drives shoreward, and your feet get soaked once again. We have no control over the timing of the tide, or the distance it travels, or its strength. We may try to be King Canute and hold it back But we cannot. Inexorably, it comes and it goes.

The moment of the returning tide in bereavement, Mike suggests, might be stimulated by a piece of music, or by a sound, or a sight. It might be a smell – perfume, cooking, roses. It might be a familiar face, or a feeling, or a sudden memory, or an event. The bond of love that matters to you is right there, as important as ever.

Agnes was an elderly woman I worked with some years ago. Her son, Tommy, had died of a brain tumour at the age of forty-one and, this being 'her baby', the youngest of five children, and because Tommy had never left home, she missed him deeply. A widow herself, Agnes talked warmly and lovingly about her memories of Tommy – 'the man of the house' – about how proud she was of her son, and about his character and personality. Our group met on a Thursday afternoon, and, as was our pattern, we had started off by reviewing what had been happening for folk during the previous week, and how they had been coping.

Agnes told us that the hardest part of the week for her had been watching Scotland play an international football match at Hampden on the previous Saturday afternoon. Tommy had been a member of the 'Tartan Army', following his beloved Scotland all over the world. Agnes liked football too and was desperate for Scotland to win. But watching them play was a bitter-sweet experience, for the excitement of the match reminded her of times she'd watched games with Tommy or seen highlights of games she knew he would be at.

'Scotland were playing well,' Agnes said, 'and got a penalty. It was crucial. I watched the player line up to take the kick. I was on the edge of my seat, muttering: "Come on Scotland! Come on Scotland!" And when the ball went in the net, I jumped to my feet and yelled, "Well done, Tommy. You've scored for Scotland. I knew you could do it!" And when I realised what I'd just said, I sank back into my chair and burst into floods of tears.'

There was a lot of emotion in the room at that moment because everyone understood perfectly what had happened. The tension was broken by one of the other women who spoke this truth: 'I'll bet you felt close to Tommy, Agnes, despite your tears.'

'Aye, I did that, lassie,' she responded, 'and I said a big thank you to my Tommy for helping Scotland get their goal.'

In the 1997 Wild Goose Publications' book *When Grief is Raw*, there are a number of wonderfully expressive hymns by John L Bell and Graham Maule. One of them is entitled *How Long, O Lord* and is based on the words of Psalm 13:

How long, O Lord, will you quite forget me?
How long, O Lord, will you turn your face from me?
How long, O Lord, must I suffer in my soul?
How long, how long, O Lord?

How long, O Lord, must this grief possess my heart?
How long, O Lord, must I languish night and day?
How long, O Lord, shall my enemy oppress?
How long, how long, O Lord?

Look now, look now and answer me, my God;
give light, give light lest I sleep the sleep of death.
Lest my enemies rejoice at my downfall,
look now, look now, O Lord.

(From *When Grief is Raw,* www.wildgoose.scot, quoted with permission.)

So the Psalmist cries out to his God. In bereavement, pain is hard to bear and the cries are deep and loud. And whether 'God-directed' or 'humanity-directed' such heart-rending cries obey no time-limits.

How are we to respond? Not by trying to give an answer, or a reason, or an explanation when there are none, but to offer the embrace of our understanding – philosophically, spiritually and physically – to those who cry out to us. We all want people's pain to go away. We wouldn't be human if we didn't. But in bereavement there isn't a 'fix' that will make everything better. It's wrong to expect that a simple intervention or explanation will bring an end to sadness. We like it when people say they're 'over it' or have 'moved on', so that we can be satisfied with what we have helped to achieve. But we can't *fix* loss. No matter how hard we try, we can't stop the tide going in and out.

When, two decades ago, this country exhibited a quite remarkable, and in many ways surprising, public reaction to the death of Princess Diana, many commentators affirmed that this indicated a fundamental change in British society's reaction to death.

'We're more open about our grief,' some said.

'The stiff upper lip has gone,' said others.

'We're more understanding and accepting than we used to be,' we were told.

And while that may be true in the public arena, where tears were acceptable, where strangers hugged strangers in their mutual sorrow, where flowers were thrown on a hearse, where a eulogy was cheered to the echo, it did not – and does not now – translate into an understanding and acceptance of private grief in personal loss.

This manifests itself in the shorter and shorter time-frame in which it is deemed acceptable to exhibit reactions to loss. There is also the insidious appearance of what I've come to call 'the pecking order of grief', where some losses are considered more challenging than others – and, therefore, more likely to create obvious signs of grieving. In addition, the noticeable diminishing of expressions of community solidarity in our current society and the parallel rise of individualism provide fewer opportunities for bereaved people to experience any normalising framework in which to process their grief. Allied to that, there is the loss of modelling in our society. Where can I see normal reactions to grief that make it OK for me to act in a similar way? And, finally, there's the 'let's get on' attitude, which all too quickly expects bereaved people to function just as they did before.

Such is the reality of a society which purports to be more open and understanding but which cannot, and does not, deliver. A measuring-stick? Not possible. A book of rules? Not available. A chart of distinctive stages? Hasn't been written. Definable norms? Never been worked out. A patient and tolerant society in which to process your bereavement? Sadly, no …

If you are bereaved, you're the only one who'll know what's right, appropriate and acceptable in your own circumstances. Check it out, of course. Talk it through. Ask your questions. But always remember that you are unique, and the journey of loss that begins with the death of someone you have known and loved in your own special way is yours alone.

Some years ago, I spoke with a church group about my work in the hospice and my role in bereavement care. In the Q&A at the end, the questions allowed me to tell some stories and deal with some fairly straightforward issues. But one woman had a query that quite took me by surprise. 'How long must I grieve?' she asked. 'My husband died eight years ago,' she said, clearly holding back her tears. 'I still cry myself to sleep some nights. Not every night, and not as often as at the start. But it doesn't feel right. Is there something wrong with me? Shouldn't I be over it by now? How long do I have to grieve?'

It was an important question – for her and for the others present – and one with which I wasn't unfamiliar. I began my response by sharing a story of my being burned as a child, when my head was covered with scalding water. It left me with a scar on my neck, which, over time, has become hard for people to see if they don't know it's there. Mostly, I don't think about it. Sometimes I see it and it bothers me a little. And occasionally, when I shave, I nick the raised skin around the scar and I bleed on my collar. I've had that burn mark for over 60 years. My life has grown round it. It's an integral part of me – and it won't ever go away.

'How long will you grieve?' I said. 'You will be bereaved for ever. Your life will grow round your loss. In time, you will accept it as part of you. You might even have periods when you forget all about it, and it doesn't bother you at all. Sometimes, you'll be faced with it again and you'll say "Damn!", because you wish it hadn't happened – just like my burn. And occasionally you'll nick yourself and bleed on your collar. Not literally,' I added quickly. 'But sometimes your grief will return with all its pain and sorrow. You'll cry yourself to sleep. You'll be a puddle on the floor at a soppy movie. You'll weep buckets at the school nativity play. You'll be angry when you see couples holding hands in the street. You'll hate Christmas. *That's* bleeding on your collar. Not all the time, but when the grief hurts – and sometimes it has to. How long do you grieve? Eight years, ten years, whatever … You're the only one that'll know.'

There is no rule book or measuring-stick for bereavement. If there is, the only one that matters is the one that a grieving woman at a church Q&A is going home to deal with and make sure she's got the measurement right for herself.

Tides

High and low, fast and slow,
in and out, they're there,
twice a day, come what may.
When it's bright and fair
tender hands stroke the sands
of my gentle shore.
But the sea frightens me
when the tempests roar.

Waves hit hard; coasts are scarred;
raging is unfurled;
wind and rain, unrestrained;
tides that change my world.
Here I stand on the land,
watching them again,
come and go; high and low;
all they bring is pain.

Gentle days, sunshine rays,
all too soon are gone.
Tides of tears, guilt and fears;
feeling overcome;
storms galore; battered shores;
threats to life and limb;
rain that stings; winds that bring
blackening skies, so grim.

Tides of grief, disbelief,
horror and despair;
tides that prey, steal away
every hope that's there.

Tides that win, rolling in,
never seem to cease.
Tides again, with disdain
shattering my peace.

When will I see a sky
blue and free of clouds?
When will I justify
standing here unbowed?
When will I modify
all my hopes and dreams?
When will I …? 'When?' I cry.
Never, child, it seems …

3. Elisabeth Kübler-Ross, *On Death and Dying* (1969), Tavistock/
    Routledge
4. Colin Murray Parkes, *Studies of Grief in Adult Life* (4th Edition,
    2010), Penguin
5. William Worden, *Grief Counselling and Grief Therapy* (4th edition
    2009), Routledge
6. Dennis Klass, Phyllis R Silverman and Steven L Nickman,
    Continuing Bonds: New Understandings of Grief (1996), Taylor
    & Francis
7. Margaret Stroebe and Henk Schut, 'The dual process model of
    coping with bereavement', *Death Studies* 1999; 23:197-224
8. For a more detailed exploration of current grief theories and their
    application to bereavement issues, see Tom Gordon, Ewan Kelly
    and David Mitchell, *Spiritual Care for Healthcare Professionals:
    Reflecting on Clinical Practice* (2011), Radcliffe

Chapter 7

Angels
with clipped wings

High up on the north side of the nave of Exeter Cathedral is a projecting balcony built in the middle of the 14th century. It is beautifully and ornately decorated and is known as the 'Minstrels' Gallery'. Along the front and sides of the gallery, set in individual alcoves, there is a series of angels playing what are clearly medieval instruments, including – so the guidebook tells us – bagpipes, harp, gittern (an ancestor of the modern guitar), shawm (a double-reeded woodwind instrument superseded by the modern oboe) and a little organ. A room behind the balcony now houses a section of the cathedral organ which allows it to be heard more effectively in the centre of the nave.

There is no doubt that the beauty, age and style of the Minstrels' Gallery adds much to the history and attraction of Exeter Cathedral. But it is the story the guide shared with us when I was being shown round the cathedral with a group of tourists that both fascinated and intrigued me. The gallery, we were told, was constructed according to the instructions of the cathedral's architects, including the correct number of alcoves for the instrument-playing angels. The angels, however, were made separately, no doubt by skilled wood-carvers, according to the information and measurements they had been given. But when it came time for the angels to be placed in their relevant positions in the Minstrels' Gallery, they didn't fit the alcoves which had been prepared for them. The width of each was correct, but most of them were too tall. The wood-carvers hadn't taken into consideration the height of the angels' wings.

What was to be done? Too much work would be wasted if the angels were discarded and another batch commissioned. Time was pressing. The Minstrels' Galley had to be fixed in its agreed position. The solution was that the sections of the angels' wings that were too tall for the alcoves were chopped off! And soon enough, all the angels – now the correct size – were placed in their apportioned positions, each one playing its instrument, each one fulfilling its role, but each and every one with clipped wings.

I was delighted that there are places in the Minstrels' Gallery in Exeter Cathedral for angels with clipped wings. Not one was rejected. None of them was deemed unfit. Oh yes, they were all flawed, less than perfect. They weren't what they once were. Yet each one had its place. Angels with clipped wings were acceptable.

There are many people I have worked with in their bereavements who, because they are not deemed to be responding predictably or acceptably to their loss, are judged to be 'problematic'. They are spurned or criticised because they do not fit preconceived expectations or readily accepted patterns of behaviour. I have lost count of the number who have told me that someone, at one time or another, has used expressions such as: 'Don't be saying things like that'; 'You shouldn't be thinking that way'; 'That's not right'. As a result they feel at best that people are not listening to or caring for them, and at worst rejected and pushed away by other people's judgementalism and dismissive attitudes. They are, if you like, angels with clipped wings, who instead of finding a place where they are accepted despite their perceived imperfections and flaws, are rejected and judged to be failures, because they 'don't fit' what's expected.

One such manifestation of this is the expression of suicidal thoughts when in the depths of despair. If you have dealt with the bereaved at all, you will have heard people say things like: 'There's no point in going on ...'; 'I go to sleep and hope I don't wake up again ...'; 'There's no purpose in life any more ...'; 'To be honest, I'd be better off dead ...' If you are bereaved yourself, you might even have expressed similar sentiments. Living with bereavement, especially in the early days and weeks, sometimes brings to the surface such negative thoughts. A sense of hopelessness, a lack of motivation, an overwhelming loss of meaning can be so hard to bear it seems like the only way out is for life to end.

How are we to react to such expressions of hopelessness? Of course, we can dismiss them or, as I have hinted above, tell people to stop it because we don't like what we hear. That's because such sentiments create feelings of panic in us. 'What if they mean it? What if it's true? What if there's something being planned?' And we will do our level best to dismiss such negativity: 'Don't say such things ...'; 'You have a lot to live for ...'; 'It can't be that bad ...'; 'Think of your grandkids ...'; and the like. In short, we have little time for the angels with clipped wings.

Perhaps the best way to begin to accept such negativity is to validate this as being an appropriate response to the devastation of loss. It's OK to feel as bad as this. Might I not feel the same if I were in their shoes?

Of course, this can be a high-risk strategy, and our response to hopelessness – even a response to our *own* hopelessness – must be handled with care, sensitivity and understanding. But I have become convinced that accepting negative thoughts as appropriate and normal is an important expression of empathy and the beginning of acceptance, tolerance and the true companionship of a fellow traveller that bereaved people surely need.

'You shouldn't feel that way or be saying such things' is dismissive of angels who don't fit the alcove we have already prepared. While 'Yes, I think I understand how hard it is for you' is accepting of the real brokenness of angels whose wings have been clipped.

When Cedric was in one of our programmes, he didn't say much in the first couple of sessions. Widowed after a long marriage, living alone, and with family some distance away, he struggled with motivation, energy and a sense of purpose, and was overwhelmed by loneliness. Every day was the same. Another grind of facing life alone. Another crippling day of loss.

We were talking about 'cooking for one' in our third session, with the help of a nutritionist, and conversation was about portion sizes and recipes, freezers and ready-meals, soups and nutritional balance. In the midst of it all, Cedric said: 'It's all very well talking about all of this. But every day I wake up I cry, and I say, "Oh shit! Another bloody day to get through!" And to be honest, I pray that I don't wake up at all …'

There was that immediate moment of natural panic in me, and I suspect in everyone. But the response from the participants wasn't to dismiss Cedric, or to tell him to stop. Instead, one of the women said, 'Thank you, Cedric. I'm glad you said that. I was thinking exactly the same.' And, within seconds, the nods of the others had turned into similar responses. In one way or another, everyone expressed an empathy with Cedric out of their own experience of the hopelessness of loss. They were all telling stories of how their angel wings had been clipped and were completely accepting of others who were in the same position.

And Cedric? He didn't say much more. He didn't need to. His vigorous nods in response to the understanding and acceptance of the others said enough. With the clipped wings of his bereavement issues, he'd found his place in the Minstrels' Gallery of support.

But there's another aspect of bereavement that's worth exploring around the 'clipped wings' issue. Fundamental to the journey of loss for *everyone* who is bereaved is the question: 'Who am I now?'

We all crave meaning and purpose in life, and for many (if not all) of us, these are built up over time in the relationships that matter to us. We talk naturally about the closeness of siblings, the warmth between parent and child, a married couple being 'as one'. And we know for ourselves that such relationships are integral to our sense of worth, and our understanding of who we are, and what we are, and where we stand in the great scheme of things. Is it any surprise, therefore, that the death of anyone with whom we have a relationship that gives us the meaning and purpose we crave destabilises us and threatens our understanding of self?

Who am I in living without my wife after fifty-two years of marriage? Who am I when my only brother has died? Who am I when at the age of twenty-two I've lost both parents? Who am I when I had two children and one of them has died? Who am I now that bereavement has irrevocably changed my perspective on life and any meaningful concept of my future?

Every loss brings searching questions of personal identity. This can affect the widow or widower after many years of marriage, or those who are bereaved of a life-partner after a very short time. 'How hard it is,' a widower said to me, 'to tick the "w" box for "widowed" on a form when for forty years it was always the "m" box I ticked for "married".' The death of a parent can bring with it a new vulnerability – even in adult life – and the loss of the second parent raises the 'orphan' issue, which someone has described to me recently as 'the ultimate in growing up'. Equally, the loss of a much-loved grandparent, child, sibling, significant relation or friend can have a destabilising effect. And what do you say in answer to the question, 'Do you have children?' when one of your four children has died, and you don't know whether to answer, 'I have four,' or 'I have three and one died,' when you may then have to tell a story you find it painful to relate? And, of course, the negative effects of loss are not confined to bereavements. Consider the effects on people of the loss of a happy family, a breach of trust, substance abuse, childlessness, redundancy, bankruptcy, natural disasters, and a host of other traumatic events. The list is endless, and you will no doubt be able to add to it from your own personal experience or the knowledge of the devastating effects of different losses on people you know.

In all of these issues, we are faced with many questions. But perhaps the most profound and overwhelming is this one: 'Who am I now?'

As carers who seek to make a difference and offer appropriate support, we can begin by accepting that these questions are appropriate in bereavement. Clarity will take time to evolve. But we can help profoundly by giving people time and space to find their own answers.

Another image comes from a different religious place, but one with which I'm even more familiar than Exeter Cathedral – the restored medieval Abbey on the island of Iona. In the east wall of Iona Abbey, set beside an arched window and looking down on the Communion Table, there are two carvings in the stone. They are in the part of the medieval abbey which was in ruins before the Abbey Church was rebuilt by the Duke of Argyll in the early part of the twentieth century, and the remains of the Abbey's living quarters restored by George MacLeod and the Iona Community between the 1930s and 1960s. Not surprisingly, the carvings are well weathered and far from clear. Yet they are distinctive enough for the reflective visitor to pick out two important symbols of the medieval monastic life – the monkey and the cat.

These two carvings point to the two sides of community life and personal devotion – the monkey, representing busyness, activity, liveliness, work, and all that makes up the 'doing' part of our lives; and the cat, restful, waiting, calm, watchful, sleeping, and all that makes up the 'peaceful' part of our lives. The activity of the monkey, and the restfulness of the cat; work and reflection;

wakefulness and rest; doing and thinking; service and prayer.

So, whenever the monks of old gathered for worship in their abbey, or stood around their altar to share the eucharist, they were below the watchful eyes of the two symbols of a life in balance – work and rest.

The destabilising effect of bereavement disrupts the natural balance of our lives. That's not to say that when we are *not* living with bereavement all of us get the balance right all of the time. Too much busyness and not enough rest can lead to burnout and breakdown. Too much reflectiveness and other aspects of the contemplative life (and, yes, there can be too much of that) can lead to an imbalance in the other direction, such that we could be mockingly described as 'too heavenly minded to be of any earthly use'.

We all struggle to find a proper balance in our daily living. But in bereavement it becomes even more so as the 'Who am I?' question raises its head. There is the inevitable lethargy, tiredness and loss of motivation. It's not that we *choose* to be still and quiet, to spend time in reflective thought or meditation and prayer. It's just that such weariness seems to be forced on us that we have no choice but to succumb to it. We might want to throw it off, to be more 'alive' than we feel, to get back to the normality of motivation, decision-making and busyness that defines the 'doing' part of our lives. But we're not in control of it all – we feel weighed down and unable to get ourselves out of the rut.

The other side of the issue is equally worrying. We can be driven into the 'doing' side of our lives, leaving no space for – or deliberately avoiding – the thinking and resting part.

I worked with a woman whose mother had died. Carla had always lived at home, and, her father having died when she was a teenager, she and her mother had become lifelong companions. In her mother's later years, Carla had taken early retirement to be what became a full-time carer. She gave her all to her mother as she knew her mother would have done for her should the roles have been reversed.

When the end came, Carla was relieved. Of course, she'd lost her best friend, her caring role, the routine, the sense of purpose that she'd had for many years. She knew that. She knew bereavement would be hard, despite her willingness to 'let mother go'. But what she wasn't ready for was the 'drivenness' and manic busyness that took over her life almost from the very start.

She'd cleaned the house from top to bottom in the week after her mother's death. People would drop in to visit, sometimes unannounced. Perhaps family would need a place to stay. And, anyway, mother had been so fastidious about the state of the house she couldn't possibly let her down. And she'd cleaned the house again from top to bottom when the funeral was done, and the people had all gone. All the places she'd cleaned already and that didn't need cleaning, she cleaned a second time. She'd gutted the kitchen – emptying all the units and washing all the casseroles, and the like – and had it 'just so', even though it had never been anything other than 'just so' in all the time she'd lived in the house. And she cleaned the kitchen again, even the places that didn't need cleaning. She didn't know why. She didn't know how to stop. So she cleaned and stayed busy. And she cleaned and never sat down. And she cleaned and didn't stop to think. And she cleaned and wore herself out with cleaning.

Carla was trapped by the 'monkey' side of her life, the 'busyness', the 'doing' part. She knew it wasn't good; that it would ultimately be destructive; that the balance would have to be restored. But she also felt powerless to do anything about it.

What Carla was living with is what many people have shared with me in their bereavement journey – especially in the early weeks and months. 'I have to keep myself busy.' 'I can't stay at home; I have to go out and keep active all the time.' 'I walk everywhere; it keeps my mind off things.' And why? Because to let go of busyness and give way to thoughtfulness, reflection and often sorrow is too much to bear, too overwhelming to contemplate. Busyness will keep the sadness at bay ... And it does, for a while, until we become so trapped in the busyness that we don't know how to relax any more.

So the truth is this: when bereavement knocks our well-being out of balance and we don't know who we really are any more, sometimes we get trapped by the cat, and the enforced weariness of bereavement causes panic and fear and threatens to overwhelm us; and sometimes we get trapped by the monkey, and the enforced (and often manic) busyness that takes over our lives gives no space or time for anything else.

Of course, there are times when weariness can lead to low mood, and low mood can be a sign of a clinical depression. And of course there are times when over-activity can be a sign of an out-of-control obsessive-compulsive issue or have some other underlying physical or mental cause. We should always be prepared to have worrying changes in our lives – physical, mental and emotional – checked out by our GP in case they are symptoms of something more problematic. And those of us who work with bereaved people should always be conscious that not everything that is different in a person's life can simply be labelled as 'because they are bereaved.' But in *general* terms the cat or the monkey can create an imbalance that is both unusual and potentially worrying for us.

Both reactions to loss are normal. Both are issues in loss which are more common than people realise or are prepared to admit. They are expected signs of the destabilising consequences of the cataclysmic effects the bereavement is having on your life. Recognising this is the beginning of coping with it and the start of a rebalancing of life between the conflicting pulls of the monkey and the cat.

Effectively it means that the struggle of bereavement and much of the associated stress arises from the fact that we are trying to find, and to live with, 'a new normal' – wings clipped; balance out of kilter; not knowing who we are any more.

The ancient philosopher Aristotle said:

It is better to rise from life as from a banquet –
neither thirsty nor drunken.

In the same vein, I would suggest that we cannot live life and journey with bereavement being *totally* a monkey or *completely* a cat. Both have their place. Both will be manifestations of the stress of loss. But neither one should dominate the other or push the other completely away.

The French artist Henri Matisse once said:

What I dream of is an art of balance,
or purity and serenity devoid of troubling and depressing
subject matter …
a soothing, calming influence on the mind,
rather like a good armchair which provides relaxation
from physical fatigue.

What I hope for in the lives of those of us who are bereaved is the same 'art of balance', and access to a good armchair which will embrace us in our weariness and sustain us sufficiently till we are ready to be active once more.

Bereavement destabilises us and threatens to destroy the familiarity of our lives and our relationships. It is confusing and troubling to know that we are different – we are those angels with clipped wings – and that everyone who is bereaved struggles with the same issue. So we will inevitably ask 'Who am I now?' as we swing this way and that in the uncertainty of finding that place where we feel ourselves stabilised again – the 'new normal'. But it will happen. Because of the bereaved people I have worked with over many years, I can say that with certainty. And as I look up at the Minstrels' Gallery in Exeter Cathedral, I don't see the clipped wings of the angels. Instead I see every angel with its allotted place, and they all look pretty good to me.

Can't

Can't stop; too much to do;
Places to be; no time for you.
Can't stop; much to achieve;
No time for me; no time to grieve.
Can't stop; must fill the space;
Rushing around; upping the pace.
Can't stop; timings to keep;
No time to think; no time to weep.

Can't move; not thinking straight;
Energy's gone; can't concentrate;
Can't move; weary and worn;
Time to be sad; always to mourn.
Can't move; losing my drive;
Making mistakes; less than alive.
Can't move; lost my intent;
Time for more tears; constant lament.

Hold on! Patience, my friend;
'Doing' will pass; tiredness will end.
'Manically busy' won't be your way;
'Weary and worn' cannot overstay.
Hold on! Time will restore
Balance again, purpose once more.
Sadness and tears? They'll have their space!
But meaning and purpose will still have a place.

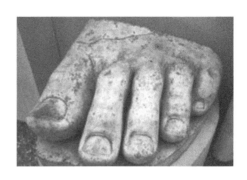

Chapter 8

Chipping away at faith

Exploring one of the many museums in the Italian city of Venice some years ago, I came across a room which displayed several parts of marble and stone statues unearthed from the rubble of ancient palaces, grand houses and city squares. Among these Roman artefacts there were damaged heads of unknown people. Some figures were more complete (many shorn of their arms which had long since been lost) whose names remained unknown. There were fragments of mosaic floors, wall decorations and carved columns.

In the middle of it all, there was one gigantic foot, about a metre in length from heel to big toe, and about half a metre across. It was all that had survived from a great statue, the signage said, probably of a god, but there was no indication of which one. Given the size of the foot, it was hard to conceptualise the magnitude of the statue in its complete form. But it must have been massive, too big to have indoors, so more than likely it would have been erected in the centre of a courtyard, or sited at the entrance to a temple, an imposing, dominating and magnificent specimen.

As I walked around this giant foot, I recalled something from my time in New College Divinity Faculty in Edinburgh back in 1970 when I was beginning my training for ministry in the Church of Scotland. I had approached my theological training with all the certainty of youth. I had been well versed in issues of faith, doctrine and scripture, from family, church, ministers, youth leaders and many of the 'heroes' of faith I sought to emulate.

My lecturer in New Testament classes in my first year was the Professor of New Testament, Hugh Anderson. Here was a man who was not only an excellent educator, but also a churchman, who saw it as part of his role as a teacher to challenge our certainties and presuppositions. It was scary, but ultimately enlightening and rewarding to me as a young student. I have never forgotten Hugh Anderson's influence on my thinking, my beliefs and, in time, my ministry.

In the midst of one of his frequent debates with some of his more intransigent students, and as a challenge to those of us who thought we knew it all and had little more to learn, Professor Hugh Anderson said this – and it was so memorable and influential that nearly fifty years later I can quote it almost word for word.

'Faith,' he said, 'is being like a skilful sculptor, with a concept, an idea, a mental picture of what your statue is going to be like. It's clear in your head. It's beautiful. But as you begin to tackle your rough-hewn block of marble, all you ever get to finish and see in its completeness is one big toe. The rest of it is there, still to be created, but it's not yet found its completed form, and may not for a while – or even ever!'

Hugh Anderson was right. We might have an image, indeed a set of beliefs, a concept of faith, that is clearly formed and will stand tall and strong above all else, while in *reality* all we ever get to see is the formation of one big toe. That doesn't invalidate what we work towards and what we ultimately wish to create, but in the real world the carving of that big toe is all that is ever likely to be clear. What is complete and sure and viewable for most of us is the big toe of one foot.

This is not a book about a religious or specifically Christian approach to bereavement issues. There are times in our bereavement groups when religion is not touched on at all. But, of course, there are also times when the conversation turns to aspects of faith.

There are those who have no faith, who admire those who do, and see in them a coping strategy they would like to have. There are others whose faith is severely challenged in the journey of loss, and sometimes completely lost. There are many who find support in their religious community. There are some who feel worse among their belief-groups and, as a result, less supported than they expected because of the attitudes of those around them. So it's worthwhile reflecting for a little while on faith issues and how an exploration of these can help with or exacerbate bereavement problems.

Horace Walpole in *Memoirs on the Reign of King George II* wrote this:

> *Perhaps those, who, trembling most, maintain a dignity in their fate, are the bravest: resolution on reflection is real courage.*

We cannot but admire those who, in the devastation of bereavement, maintain a dignity and a resolve above and beyond what might be expected. There is something brave we see in others who, despite the trembling they might experience in other places and at other times, appear to be dealing with their loss in a stoical and courageous fashion, and whose faith underpins that approach.

Problems arise, however, when people who are bereaved feel they *must* exhibit such bravery and dignity because they have a Christian or other religious perspective, believing that to do otherwise is to be diminished in the eyes of the faith community and even to be less agreeable in the sight of their God. We hope people will be honest about their struggles with loss. That's what our bereavement work is predicated upon. But it's a struggle to be honest about faith when we feel we should be stronger and more dignified in bereavement because of our beliefs, and even that we've failed because we have doubts and questions.

As I've explored earlier, one of the hardest things to bear in grief and loss is the attitude of some people that they know better than we do about how we should be coping with loss. Comments such as 'You should be over it by now …' and 'What do you mean it's still hard? You've had months to deal with it …' and 'You should have moved on …' offer little empathy for and understanding of those who are bereaved.

When we add to this our *own* perception, along the lines of 'If I had a stronger faith, I would be coping better than this,' it makes reality even more difficult to live with and express. So is it any surprise that people who expected their faith – and their God – to sustain them in times of trouble, and whose reality is devastation and hopelessness, feel that their faith clearly wasn't good enough to begin with, or that their faith – or their God – has failed them just at the time when they needed it the most?

And the response to that? Faith is sometimes rejected. The faith community abandoned. Or people live a lie … they might be trembling inside, but they are damned sure they're not going to admit that to anyone else.

I worked with a woman in the hospice whom I knew only as Miss Stepney. She never offered me her first name, and it didn't really matter. She knew I was a chaplain, and I knew she'd gone to church regularly. Or at least she *had* when her mother was alive. And they'd always gone together. But now, several months after her mother's death, Miss Stepney hadn't gone back.

She didn't consider herself a brave woman. She trembled more than she wanted to, especially when she was out and about and people asked her how she was. And that was especially true about going to church. She'd gone the Sunday after her mother's funeral. It was part of her routine, as it had been for her and her mother and grandmother before that. But it was just too hard. She cried through the whole act of worship. She wasn't sure she could go back. But what would people think of her when she stopped going? Could she live with herself? Well, she just had to.

But, for some reason she could never explain, about six months after her mother's death she decided she had to give it another go. Dignity, courage, or whatever, would have to be shown in huge quantities. The 'trembling' part would have to be left at home or kept hidden as best as she was able.

She kept her cool as she parked her car at the church gate. She composed herself as she walked up the path. She took a deep breath as she approached the church door. And there stood the vicar, welcoming people to worship. 'Miss Stepney,' the vicar said with glee, 'very nice to see you. How are you after all this time?'

'Not too bad, Vicar?' *Dignity* …

'We've missed you, been worried about you.' *Sympathy* …

'Oh, I've been doing OK … Things to do, you know?' *Courage* …

'Well it's good to have you back …' *Support* …

Silence … *Bravery* …

But the vicar wasn't done. 'I was just thinking the other day that your mother had had a cracking innings. She'd got well past her three-score-years-and-ten. Early nineties, wasn't it? A long and happy life.' *Dismissive* …

'Not long enough,' Miss Stepney murmured. *Truthfulness* …

But the vicar wasn't listening. 'It was her time, all part of God's plan, something we all have to come to accept …' *What?*

When Miss Stepney came to that part of her story with me, I couldn't hold back my surprise. 'Goodness me! And how did you respond to that?' I asked.

'Respond? I had nothing to say. And I'm too small and not brave enough to punch him. So I turned on my heel and headed back down the church path, leaving him open-mouthed. I sat and cried in my car for ages, and when I went home I was so angry I slammed the lounge door so hard that I broke the glass.'

Whether the vicar had a complete, gigantic statue of faith, no one will ever know. But that's what he *portrayed* to a frail, trembling, searching soul who was only at the big toe stage – or perhaps even less than that! Miss Stepney needed to be met where she was, not where the vicar – with all his clarity and certainties – expected her to be.

I don't know whether Miss Stepney ever went back to church after that. I suspect not. Personally, I would reckon that she's better off staying at home on a Sunday and, with trembling hand, continuing to chip away at the big toe of her faith.

Alfred Lord Tennyson, in *In Memoriam A.H.H. 96, ll. 11-12*, wrote this:

> *There lives more faith in honest doubt*
> *Believe me,*
> *Than in half the creeds.*

I hope Miss Stepney realised that and learned to be comfortable with it. Indeed, I'm quite sure she did!

I instanced the hymn *How Long, O Lord?* from *When Grief Is Raw* by Graham Maule and John L Bell in an earlier chapter. 'How long?' is so often the heart-rending cry of people who are bereaved as they look for a clear timescale for their grief. Here's another hymn from the same publication[9] – *What shall we pray?* A footnote offers us this thought:

> *In Scotland, Remembrance Sunday, when the nation honours those who have died in war, can be a fraught occasion. It brings back unspeakably painful memories to some, offends others and puzzles younger people who have only seen pictures of war. In this song, representatives of a local congregation [in this case, Carnwadric Parish Church Worship Group in Glasgow*

*along with John Bell] identified the different people who would
be reacting to services of remembrance, holding them together
before God with the same prayer.*

The hymn itself reads like this:

*What shall we pray for those who died,
those on whose death our lives relied,
silenced by war but not denied,
God give them peace.*

*What shall we pray for those who mourn,
friendships and love, their fruit unborn?
Though years have passed, hearts still are torn;
God give them peace.*

*What shall we pray for those who live
tied to the past they can't forgive,
haunted by terrors they relive?
God give them peace.*

*What shall we pray for those who know
nothing of war, and cannot show
grief or regret for friend or foe?
God given them peace.*

*What shall we pray for those who fear
war, in some guise, may reappear
looking attractive and sincere?
God give them peace.*

*God give us peace and, more than this,
show us the path where justice is;
and never let us be remiss
working for peace that lasts.*

Suspend your religious certainties or prejudices, and hear this heart-rending cry: *What shall we pray for those who mourn, friendships and love, their fruit unborn? Though years have passed, hearts still are torn; God give them peace.* Though years have passed, grief still hurts. Though years have passed, mourning still matters. Though years have passed, bereavement remains. Though years have passed …

Someone once said to me, 'People seem so sure about what I should do, and how I should think, and when I should feel this or that. But they're not inside my head. They're not inside my grief. I don't need their "so-called" expertise. I just need their willingness to listen and understand.'

This came through to me forcibly after a meeting of a group for which I was responsible in the hospice bereavement service. It had been an amicable discussion, until the topic turned to religion, and how having a faith helped, or didn't help, the grief journey. I won't go into how the discussion went – only to say that one man was very forceful in his opinion that, because he had a Christian faith which had been a mainstay for him in his ability to cope with his bereavement, it would be better – much better – if everyone else had that faith too. Indeed, it would be especially good if people believed what he believed and were able to describe their faith the way he did.

After the group, and as we were washing up the teacups, one of the participants – a dignified, quiet-spoken and sensitive woman – took me aside and said this: 'If you put that man in my group again, I'll walk out. What right has *he* to say how I should cope with my grief? Let him apply his faith to his own, but don't let him assume it will make a blind bit of difference to me. Let him go and peddle his religion somewhere else, and not force it on me.'

What the man was offering was a perspective on his abilities – and, indeed, successes – in processing his own grief. But the ways in which he expressed that only served to put a massive barrier between him and someone else. He had given the impression he was an expert in the woman's grief, when what she needed was to be listened to and understood with empathy. But what *he* wanted, what made him feel secure and that he was doing a good job, was for her to come into his world. Then, he believed, all would be well. Meanwhile, what *she* wanted and needed was for him to divest himself of his certainties and come into *her* world, where they could share the pain together.

Some years ago, I attended a national conference in Scotland on spiritual care and chaplaincy. In an imaginative way, the organisers had invited a Scottish artist and designer, Graham Ogilvie[10], to record the proceedings in pictures and not in words. So, throughout the day, Graham would take phrases or ideas that contributors had shared with the conference and draw cartoons on large sheets of paper. As the day wore on, the conference venue was filled with these cartoons, and the buzz of chat around them at the break-times was more than I'd ever found at a conference before. Later, by way of compiling a 'report' on the conference, the cartoons were 'tidied up', coloured and published. It was an exciting, stimulating and creative way of capturing the essence of what the conference had offered.

One cartoon I recall had its birth in a section of the conference around 'empathy'. A speaker had said, 'We need to be real with people, and not hide behind our protective shell of certainties.' So Graham Ogilvie drew a picture of a patient in a hospital bed, looking very forlorn, with a nurse, in uniform, standing beside her. The nurse was, however, inside a suit of armour, shielding her from the patient, so that all the patient could see was the armour-encased professional coming to the bedside. But the suit of armour was open at the back, and the nurse was easing herself out of it so that she could be the real person she needed to be with the distressed patient. In time, she would escape fully from her suit of armour and be more human and honest with her patient.

We say that 'a picture paints a thousand words'. In his novel, *Fathers and Sons*, written in 1862, Ivan Turgenev has one of his characters say:

> *The drawing shows me at one glance what might be spread over ten pages in a book.*

Graham Ogilvie showed us the truth of that during the conference. Who needs pages and pages of a conference report – which is often never looked at again – when the essence can be captured in pictures or drawings? Is it any wonder that I can remember this key point from a conference which took place decades ago while many words I've heard in more recent times have already been erased from my memory? (And, who knows, perhaps the use of images and metaphors in a book such as this began right there ...)

Whatever our role as carers, wherever empathy is needed, we can all wear our suits of armour. Nurses and chaplains, doctors and social workers, ministers and welfare staff ... we all do it, some of us more than others. We protect ourselves from the pain in front of us by encasing ourselves in our certainties and outer persona. And it may be that what the needy person sees is *only* the suit of armour and never the real 'you'.

That's seldom more obvious than in religious discussions and care. Too often I, for one, have shown the armour-plating of my certainties when I should have said, 'I just don't know.' On too many occasions, for my own protection, I've hidden myself in a protective shell because I didn't know how to engage at a human level with the pain and suffering in front of my eyes. All too readily I would portray that I had all the answers (or if I didn't, I would make sure that it sounded as if I did) when what was needed was a genuine engagement with someone's lostness and distress.

Hugh Anderson was right. We have enough trouble working on the big toe of our statue of faith without anyone else telling us how pathetic we are when they appear to have the grandest statue you've ever seen.

We need more honesty. We need to learn to be more comfortable with the big toe which is still being carved into the shape we want it to be. Or, in Graham Ogilvie's imagery, we need to come out from behind our suit of armour and start being real.

When someone says, 'Everyone's an expert in my grief – except me!', what they are saying, in effect, is that they don't need experts who come with their own certainties, but people who will listen and not talk about themselves; who will hear the pain and see the tears and not run away; who will take time, and more time, to keep contact even when other folk have stopped bothering. Bereaved people need those who will wait, and wait some more, until purpose and new directions emerge.

Chris Jones, himself widowed for ten years, is one of the resource people who works in our bereavement support programmes. In the penultimate session of every programme, Chris shares his story of loss and the journey of bereavement on which he is still travelling. He is open and honest, engaging and insightful, helpful and aware, and often very amusing indeed. And, among other things to which he returns on a regular basis, he always says that in bereavement you learn who your friends *really* are. There are many from whom you expect support and it doesn't come through. There are those who promise undying loyalty and availability who quickly fade away. There are those who are all too ready to advise and direct. But, says Chris, thank God there are some who take you by surprise, who deliver what you didn't expect, by waiting and watching, by listening and loving, and all over a longer period than anyone could ever have expected to be necessary.

I'm unhappy with a faith structure that becomes so pure that there is no room for doubts or questions. In my fifteen years as a hospice chaplain, my faith was stripped down and reformed. At one and the same time it became much simpler and much stronger. As Kathy Galloway, theologian and former leader of the Iona Community, has said, 'I believe in less and less, but the less and less I believe in, I believe in more and more.' I would echo that. If the big toe of my faith is clear, and all that's beyond it is still being worked on, that's enough for me.

This is what I wrote about it some years ago. It is, if you like, a 'creedal statement' I am happy to stand by.

> *There lives more faith in honest doubt*
> *than ever dwelt in half the creeds*
> *that tell us what we must believe – and why!*
> *For doubt is integral to faith,*
> *no matter what we're told, or read*
> *in all the books, in all the world. So try*
> *to start with honesty, and find*
> *you need no certainties to show*
> *that faith still works for you. Be real!*
> *Your questions are OK for you!*
> *It's fine to say, 'I just don't know.'*
> *Be comfortable with who you are, and feel*
> *you are just what you need to be,*
> *and if that means you're still not sure*
> *what's right or wrong or good or bad – or why! –*
> *just wait, and with your patience know*
> *this faith of yours is still secure.*
> *The truth is – only doubters need apply.*

There is no 'one size fits all' approach to issues of faith. There is no statue that can be replicated again and again. There is no suit of armour that is the ultimate protection against all pain and suffering. Like faith, bereavement is a personal journey, and what bereaved people need the most is to be given time, and space, and patience, and genuine companionship and empathy, to determine their own pathway to the future.

Please ... or pleas?

Please, wait a while; don't try to give advice.
I've heard it all before, and, though it's nice
To have a friend who tries to care for me,
I don't need told what I should do or be,
Or how I should behave, or when to smile ...
Just wait a while.

Please, stay with me; don't feel obliged to know
What feelings I might have, where I should go
Within my mind to find the peace and rest
I crave, the comfort that's my lonely quest.
Don't say you understand – that's not the key!
Just stay with me.

Please, be yourself; don't try to say what's right,
And offer clever words that cast a light
On all my darkness and my deep despair,
For you will never know what lingers there
And even when I still seem far from well ...
Just be yourself.

Please, give me time; when others promised, then
Reneged, and left me on my own again,
To face a scary world; when I was low,

And had no clue which way was best to go,
Which paths to take, what hills I had to climb ...
Just give me time.

Know love's enough; don't doubt yourself when I
Don't seem to recognise how hard you try
To wait and wait, and never say a word,
And feel such silence is, in truth, absurd.
But even when your comfort I rebuff ...
Your love's enough.

9.   From *When Grief is Raw*, www.wildgoose.scot, quoted with permission.
10. http://www.ogilviedesign.co.uk/

Chapter 9

Towards
a new normality

Over the years of our marriage, my wife and I have had a series of dogs. In truth, it's my wife who's had the dogs. I've just derived vicarious pleasure from a succession of canine pets who have joined our family. A Border collie; a rescue terrier; a springer spaniel; a saluki/spaniel cross; a working cocker. They have all been a delight to be with and in their own unique ways they have brought joy to our home.

I'm not a dog psychologist, and I don't steep myself in vet programmes on TV or follow documentaries on dog-training and behaviour traits. But I know what I know, and I see what I see. So, after forty-three years observing the subtleties of canine behaviour, I think I have a fair understanding of where they're at.

Take, for example, the strange behaviour of a dog turning round and round in a circle, one way then the other, before it settles down in its chosen spot on the hearthrug or in its bed. Sometimes it's quick, and occasionally it takes a while. Often, it's clockwise, then anticlockwise, then clockwise again. And then, once the resting place is ready, the dog curls up in a ball, happy, settled and ready for a good sleep. Why does a dog do this? I'm assured it's instinctive, a throwback to flattening grass to lie on when they were out in the wild. But there's no grass to flatten in my lounge, and the fireside rug isn't spiky and uncomfortable So, why? Maybe one day I'll ask my dog. And maybe one day she might tell me.

Then you have canine eating habits. Every dog we've ever had has been driven by food. Our current cocker spaniel has an inbuilt clock which tells her, usually to the minute, that it's feeding time. And if we haven't noticed that it's coming up to 10pm, she'll find her Kong, drop it at our feet and plead with her eyes, a pathetic whine and obvious body-language for a late-evening treat. ('Kong?', you ask? I suggest you enquire of a dog-owner …) And have you ever seen a dog savour their food, or are they not more inclined to wolf it down (note the metaphor …) as if they hadn't been fed for weeks? And I'll bet you've discovered that most dogs don't lie uninterestedly in the corner when you're cooking, but constantly poke around under your feet in case the merest morsel falls on the floor. A dog, it appears, is never full. It will eat even when it's just eaten. It will gorge on anything it finds, even if it's had enough already.

It's a 'wild dog' throwback thing again, I'm told. In the times when food was scarce, and what was available had to be eaten without recourse to care and attention, a dog – or, indeed, a pack of dogs – would eat what was available when it was available, no matter what. They can't stop themselves now. It's all instinctive, we're told. It's in the doggy genes. It's unconscious behaviour. Familiar patterns, only slightly varying due to breed-type or modified by training, are exhibited in most dogs in most families in most ages of history.

So … what am I to make of one of our dogs, Dileas (pronounced 'Jeelas', the Gaelic for 'faithful'), who paid scant attention to the turning-round-and-round-to-flatten-the-grass ritual but would lie in the hallway with her backside and adjoining rear legs halfway up the wall? To find a cool spot in a centrally-heated house? Or just to show us that she could?

Or what of Rumble, our friend's golden Labrador, who would look at food with what would appear to be complete disdain, flop down beside his bowl and stare contemptuously at his evening meal for a while before deigning to nibble at the repast his owner had placed in front of him?

Were Dileas and Rumble exhibiting their independence, bucking the trend, taking on human characteristics? (Though I may from time to time have looked with disdain at a plate of food placed in front me, I've never, as far as I can recall, slept on the floor with my backside halfway up a wall.) I'll need to watch some vet programmes on TV or take in some more documentaries on canine behaviour before I get the definitive answers to such searching questions. But I think it's got something to do with each dog being the dog it has to be. Its behaviour is neither right nor wrong. It may not fit expected patterns, and it may take its unsuspecting owner by surprise. But it's no more or less than that dog being the dog it has to be.

In bereavement, we look for familiar patterns of behaviour and reactions to loss. Such patterns can be 'linear' – as with the 'stages of grief' model explored earlier. Or they can be more flexible while still being deemed to 'fit' expected traits and characteristics of the grief journey. We aren't dogs, of course, and yet we too are driven by our psyche to respond to a particular stimulus, or event, or trauma in a particular way. So we look for that familiarity to assure ourselves that we, or others about whom we are concerned, are responding normally to bereavement issues.

Why is it, then, that we become so anxious about differences of behaviour when people are bereaved? We worry, for example, about people who don't cry at funerals or haven't apparently 'broken down' for a while thereafter. 'It's not hit her yet,' we say, almost as a criticism. 'He needs to let it all out,' we remark, in a judgemental way. We express anxiety about what we consider to be the detrimental effects of suppressing grief as the bereavement journey continues. And why? Because *we* have decided, in our infinite knowledge of such things, what's 'normal', so that when people who are bereaved don't react in ways that we perceive to be the predictable patterns, we judge or criticise, or label them as 'problematic'.

What of the widow who continues to set a place at the kitchen table for many months after her husband's death? And what of the man who goes every day to weep by his twin sister's grave – even in the worst of weathers – and does so for months and months? Or what of the mother who leaves her daughter's room exactly the way it was when the eighteen-year-old went off to college only to be killed in a fatal RTA? And what of the widower who carries his wife's handbag with him when he goes out, and sits it on the passenger seat beside him while he's driving, and tells his wife everything that's going on – even asking her for advice?

Out of the norm? Well, perhaps, though I'm quite sure you will have your own stories to tell of behaviours in bereavement, in your own life or in the life of someone you know well, which seem equally strange. But bizarre, problematic, 'sleeping on the hall floor with your backside half way up the wall' kind of stuff? I don't think so.

It's important that manifestations of grief are normalised. But when we don't know what 'normal' is, we question whether our reactions, or those of other people, are appropriate or not. Normality, therefore, has to be checked out and responded to with reassurance both from professionals and from the experiences of others who are bereaved and react in the same way.

In bereavement – whether we are directly affected or offering support in a caring role – it is important that we seek to adjust our parameters and widen our pre-programmed spectrum of normality. When we're trained to recognise abnormalities, we'll look for them first and so *narrow* our understanding of the ways people react to loss. But when we widen our parameters, better support is possible.

When my mother died, my father was still working. For many years he and my mother had holidayed in the summer with a couple from Leeds – Ken, an old RAF pal of my dad's from World War II, and his wife, Rosaline. When Rosaline died and Ken was left a widower, my mum and dad would still go to stay with him in Leeds or take him with them to their favourite hotel in Jersey. And when Ken became quite frail, they would wheel him about in his wheelchair as old pals do. After my mother died, however, my dad didn't go on holiday for a number of years. He tried (he told me years later), but he couldn't face it without my mum. Even the pull of Leeds and Jersey, and being with his mate – two widowers together – wasn't enough to take him away from home. It was just too hard for him to go on holiday on his own. So, he didn't.

Aware of this in my father's bereavement, I was taken aback when I spoke recently with Archie, six months after his wife, Blanche, had died. I'd known Archie and Blanche for several years, and I had been saddened to hear of Blanche's death. They had no children, and I wondered how Archie would cope. I hadn't been in touch with him, so I was pleased when we met to be able to offer him my support and to have the opportunity of checking out how things were progressing for him.

Archie and Blanche had been married eleven years or so before Blanche had succumbed to ovarian cancer at the age of thirty-nine. Archie had been devastated, of course, though, given what I knew of him and the way he'd exhibited typical strength of character in the early stages of his loss, I wasn't unduly concerned about how he'd cope. However, when I enquired how things were six months on and he told me he hadn't gone back to work yet, I was just a little bit worried. But it's when he went on to tell me why that I got the real shock. He explained that he'd set himself the task of visiting *every* place in the UK that he and Blanche had spent a holiday in the fifteen years they'd known each other. All that had to be completed, he said, before he could contemplate getting back to work or dealing with any other kind of 'going forward' issue. It was an understatement to say that I was surprised.

'Why would you do that?' I asked.

'So I can be close to Blanche,' Archie replied.

'But it must be *so* hard,' I continued.

'It's all of that,' he said.

'And has it been helpful?' I enquired further.

'Yes, it has,' was Archie's surprising response. 'Yes, it has. Because, quite frankly, I needed to go to these places and to cry. I needed to cry, and to cry sore. I needed to be in touch with the pain inside me of losing the love of my life … and that was the best way I had of doing so.'

My dad came immediately to my mind. There was no way *he* could go *anywhere* on holiday, far less visit the places where he and my mum had shared happy times together. So, I wondered what torture Archie was putting himself through in this extended pilgrimage of pain. I felt for him in the agonies he was facing. I doubted whether such a process could ever be helpful. To be honest, I questioned its normality and doubted whether Archie had chosen the right path in his loss.

But what did I know? Not a lot, it appeared, or at least not enough to realise that my father's way *and* Archie's were perfectly valid *for them* … My father wasn't Archie and Archie wasn't my father. Each of them had faced a major issue in their loss and had chosen to deal with it in diametrically opposite ways. What worked for my father wouldn't have worked for Archie. And what worked for Archie *certainly* wouldn't have worked for my dad.

There is no rule book, no set formula, no standard equations that can be applied to every situation, for every person, in every generation, with every bereavement. Different factors have to be applied. Varied circumstances have to be taken into consideration.

Unique personalities and relationships have to be given their place.

The issue is not whether there is an absolute in this given situation or that which gives us a right way or a wrong way we must adopt. What really matters is whether we are being true to ourselves, and whether, having thought things through, we can say, 'This is right for me.' It's about working towards a new normality.

Leonard hadn't yet got his head round disposing of his wife's clothes. He didn't need the space, he told me, and for ages he didn't have either the motivation or emotional energy to go through his wife's things. So he'd decided it could wait. 'I'll get around to it eventually,' was his attitude, 'when it feels it's the right time.' That was fine for Leonard. He'd worked out what was right for him. He had to decide for himself. It wasn't fine, however, for Leonard's daughter. Six months after her mother's death, knowing that her father hadn't tackled the clothes, she was worried about him.

'He's stuck,' she told me. 'It's creepy, keeping all my mum's things. You'd think he'd be ready by now. I need to see him moving on. And all I see is him wallowing in self-pity and not doing what he should be doing. When will he get better?'

Leonard's daughter is, sadly, typical of many people within family circles who look at how someone is reacting to a loss and say, 'That's not the way to do it. It's not normal. If I was them I would …' So I had a conversation with Leonard about his daughter's concerns. What she'd said to me she'd also said to him, he told me – but, sadly, the spirit of concern came over as an attitude of criticism. 'She's doin' ma head in!' he said, expressing his daughter's judgements in the language of the vernacular.

'Do you keep the clothes as a kind of "default" position,' I asked him, 'you know, simply because it's easier not to do anything about it than get round to tackling it?'

He smiled and said, 'No! I keep the clothes on purpose, for now anyway. I need them to be there, because they remind me o' the wife. Indeed – and you've no tae breathe a word o' this tae ma lassie – sometimes Ah take a blouse frae a hanger an' haud it tae ma face so Ah can smell the wife's perfume.'

Did Leonard ever get around to putting his wife's clothes into a charity shop? He did – in his own time, when it was right for him. Did he hold on to a couple of special blouses so that he could look at them and feel himself close to his wife? He did – for only he would know the significance and importance of what those things meant to him. Did he ever tell his daughter he holds his wife's blouse to his face so he can smell her perfume? He never did and never will – for fear that she might not see this as normal behaviour, and go on 'doin' his head in '…

One of the sessions in our bereavement support groups focuses on issues of health and nutrition, and all that goes with 'looking after yourself' following the trauma of a death. Kellie Anderson, who works with people in the *Maggie's Centre* in Edinburgh, is our usual resource person for that topic, and she sensitively guides people through issues of eating well, exercise, dealing with stress, bodily functions, and much more besides. She also talks helpfully about how bereavement has affected her own life, and often refers to 'food tasting like cardboard' in the early stages of her bereavement, an image which never fails to elicit nods of recognition from participants in the group.

In one of the groups, we were exploring 'cooking for one', a balanced diet, cooking for two and freezing half of it for later, shopping carefully, portion-control, avoiding BOGOF offers and other issues relating to self-care. In the middle of it all, Sean, a middle-aged widower, offered this *cri de cœur*, not in a critical or dismissive way, but in absolute honesty, for it was a cry of the heart right enough.

'It's all very well talking about cooking and wastage and balanced diets and stuff, but my problem is shopping in the first place. I always did it with my wife. It was our time together, choices, plans, experimenting. It may surprise you to hear this, because I actually enjoyed the shopping expeditions. And now? Mary isn't there. Where is the pleasure in shopping alone? I can't even go into the local supermarket now, I miss her so much.'

There was pleasure in sharing. And that pleasure had gone. There was normality in shopping for two. And that normality had gone. There was purpose in planning and achieving. And that normality had gone. And now, for Sean, it was necessity without pleasure, being alone and feeling far from normal, having little purpose in caring for himself.

There's much in bereavement that's about finding a workable life – as Sean was experiencing big time – when we don't really want to or have the energy to try. You yearn for what's familiar, not just in terms of 'home' and shopping, but in other ways too. Familiar patterns, familiar timings, familiar places, familiar layouts, familiar things to look at, and touch, to be surrounded with. It's natural. It's secure. It's safe. But what was normal before isn't normal now, so a new normality has to be explored. And what transpires to be a new normality for one person may not be what's normal for someone else.

One of the fraught questions which we often turn to relates to the disposing of the ashes of a loved one. In a generation in which cremations are much more common, there is the obvious issue of the value of a headstone at a cemetery as a place of focus, and the corresponding need regarding the place in which the ashes are laid to rest – an internment with an appropriate headstone; a plaque in the crematorium Garden of Rest; a tree or bush in a woodland area; an inscription in a Book of Remembrance. But what if there is no obvious place for the ashes to go, or there are several places? And what if there are differing views or conflicting opinions within a family? Or what if nobody can make up their mind for ages?

There are as many decisions which are the out-working of these dilemmas as there are people with whom I've worked. I could fill a whole chapter with what people have decided – from the expected to the bizarre. But the simple truth is this: the end-products vary so widely, there is no 'one-size-fits-all' approach, and certainly no definitive time-scale. Each person is an individual, so the normality of their approach to the ashes issue will require a personal exploration and set of decisions, and tolerance and understanding from the rest of us.

Let me conclude this chapter with a lighter story which has been shared many times in our bereavement groups. In exploring this 'new normality' with Kellie in one session, around hints and tips about cooking and the like, the conversation got round to the use of a slow-cooker as a help for those who were still at work and had to come home at the end of the day and start cooking for themselves or their family. One of the participants, Fraser, a young man whose wife had died suddenly, leaving him to care for a teenage daughter, jumped at the idea, and resolved to invest in a slow-cooker for himself. The next week he told us, with much glee, that he had bought one, was looking forward to trying it out, and would tell us the following week how he'd got on. So, the obvious question when he arrived a week later was, 'Well, how did it go?'

'Ah,' said Fraser, 'pretty well OK. I got all the stuff, read the instructions, put it all together, took my lass to school, picked her up at the end of the day, and we were both dead excited at the prospect of a smell wafting from the kitchen when we got home, and diving in to a great pot-roast right away. And when we got home? Nothing! No smell! Not in the hallway, or in the kitchen. 'Cause I'd forgotten to switch the bloody thing on!'

There was a burst of laughter. It was a lovely moment. Fraser had tried a new normality – and had got it wrong. But he would try again – and get it right. And we would all smile again with pleasure at his success as much as we'd been at one with him when it hadn't gone right.

So if our current dog takes on the characteristics of the last one and chooses to sleep with her backside halfway up the lounge wall, I'll just have to say, 'Well, if it's OK for her, it must be OK.' And if she doesn't – then *we* have to learn that this normality is OK too!

Decisions

What'll I do with the ashes
now that the old man has gone?
Where should I scatter the ashes?
Where does he really belong?
Down on the beach in the sand dunes?
Up on the hill where he climbed?
Or should we go down to the bar of *The Crown*
where the old man spent most of his time?

What'll I do with the ashes
now that my purpose has died?
Where to dispose of the ashes?
Why's it so hard to decide?
Leave them behind and forget them?
Pretend that I never had dreams?
Or should I explore being hopeful some more,
and start work on some other schemes?

What'll I do with the ashes
now that my years have gone by –
The ashes of promises broken;
the suffering; the tears that I cried?

Go on being haunted by failure,
and still be cast down by despair?
Or should I let go of my pain, and still know
there are better days, just over there?

What'll I do with the ashes?
How will I ever adjust?
Why am I weak and uncertain;
no longer strong and robust?
When will decisions get easier?
When will my mind become clear?
When will I be sure it's the time to decide?
Please, when will the right way appear?

Oh, what'll I do with the ashes
now that my head's in a mess?
Where should I scatter the ashes?
Where is the place that is best?

Lay them aside where you want to;
wait till your thinking gets straight.
I promise you this … when the scattering's done
there's more of your life that awaits.

Chapter 10

Writing it down!

I know it's a point of debate these days, but I believe that social media is a gift that keeps on giving in our current society. I'm not a 'tweeter', but I am a regular user of Facebook. For me Facebook is one of the most important tools of communication that we have available to us. Like all social media platforms, it can be misused, and I'm as irritated as everyone else when it is utilised to share a photo of someone's lunch, or offers an outlet for extreme views, or is full of adverts for things I don't need or campaigns in which I'm not interested. But when a good friend takes me and others on a journey of discovery – from a trip of a lifetime to sharing worries around illness or hospital treatment – then, for me, a social media platform such as Facebook fulfils its proper role.

Another obvious example of using a media platform through which we can share our thoughts is 'blogging'. I started doing a daily blog* at the beginning of the first Covid-19 lockdown in March 2020. I only intended to do this for a short time, but as I now offer 'A Thought for the Day' on a regular basis, I've come to realise that blogging is an important part of my writing and the processing of my thoughts. And I do like reading blogs, and being stimulated by ideas, research, comments and challenging thoughts from people who have got something decent to say and who write well.

---

* https://swallowsnestnet.wordpress.com

The truth is Facebook, blogs, recording our thoughts, keeping a journal, composing an email, writing to a friend, or even jotting down random ideas and concepts, is worthwhile for the writer even before anything is read by anyone else. There is great benefit in making personal writing a regular activity.

A recent report in the *Academy of Management Journal* tells us that in an experiment with sixty-three recently unemployed professionals, those assigned to write about their thoughts and emotions surrounding the loss of their job were re-employed more quickly than those who wrote about non-traumatic topics or who didn't write at all. 'Expressive writing,' says the article's abstract, 'appeared to influence individuals' attitudes about their old jobs and about finding new employment rather than their motivation to seek employment.'[11]

Laura King writing in the *Personality and Social Psychology Bulletin*[12] talks about work she did with undergraduates who were randomly assigned to write about their most traumatic life event, their best possible future self, both of these topics or a non-emotional control topic, for twenty minutes each day for four consecutive days. Mood was measured before and after writing, and three weeks later measures of subjective well-being were obtained. The findings emphasised that writing about life-goals was significantly less upsetting than writing about trauma and was associated with a significant increase in subjective well-being. Five months into the study, it was clear that the positive effects for the participants of writing about themselves, their emotional issues and future aspirations, continued to be of as much benefit as writing about a trauma.

What this simple study seems to be saying is this: it's not just the traumas of life we need to reflect on. We have known for a long time the benefit people gain from thinking through, writing about and exploring the problem areas of their lives. But when we have the opportunity to think, write, verbalise or share about *any* aspect of our lives in an ordered, constructive and supported fashion there is much to be gained.

I'm not a management consultant, or a psychologist, or a researcher, but I know what I know: that in bereavement the benefits of writing are equally applicable. Whether it's reflecting on the trauma of the death or hopes and dreams for the future, recording immediate feelings or exploring issues over a longer period of time, making lists of decisions to be tackled or things achieved ... taking time to explore any kind of expressive writing is clearly beneficial.

As we saw earlier, there is benefit in being encouraged to talk and to know you are being listened to. But there are many times in our bereavement groups when articulation of feelings or relating part of a life story isn't easy. People stumble over their words, or talk in a jumbled kind of way, or literally can't speak because of their emotion. So it may well be that it is *afterwards*, in the privacy of a home or a coffee shop or a bus journey, that they are able to form words more clearly. That's when writing things down can be a useful part of the bereavement journey. It serves to anchor our thoughts, clarify ideas and articulate feelings, and may even be a preparation for a clearer sharing next time around.

I have worked with some people who have taken this one stage further, and written a letter to their deceased loved one – sometimes to be placed in the coffin with them or dropped into the grave; often completed, sealed and left with their own personal papers – to express their yearnings, to pour out their sorrow, or even to say all the important things that had been left unsaid before the end because the death was so sudden.

Let me instance two such benefits of writing things down as part of a bereavement journey. Before the days of civil partnership and same-sex marriage legislation, Glenn and Alan were in a gay relationship which they kept hidden from their families. Social standing, family relationships and even employment prospects would all, to their mind, have been severely compromised if their sexuality was 'outed'. So for many years they kept their relationship private. And even though they lived every day with the apprehension that the 'truth would out', they continued to share a deep and committed relationship. Alan died in the hospice when I worked there. Glenn had been nurtured with great sensitivity by the hospice staff – with whom he and Alan had been honest about their circumstances – and he had been given privacy, time and space with Alan right up to the moment when Alan died. The 'anticipatory grief' of his loss was both well understood and responded to by a caring staff team.

We had, however, no control over what happened afterwards. For Glenn, the death of his life-partner was one thing, but he had no public role for his grief and no obvious support from others – because no one knew the depth of his sorrow. But it was writing that got him through it. He kept a journal; he wrote letters to Alan; he sent emails to me. He took time to explore his pain, his thoughts, his sorrow – and all to his benefit.

If, as I suggested earlier, part of the role of a hospice chaplain is to help people 'articulate their longings', the same is true of bereavement work. In sharing and in private writing, if people can learn how to articulate their issues, good comes from that process.

Because Glenn had no public role in Alan's funeral or wake, he decided to set up a memorial to the love of his life. So he contacted the local council and had them put up a bench at a viewpoint overlooking his village. While the bench was being secured to its concrete base, he dropped a letter he'd written to Alan into the foundations, and he knew that his words would always be there. I don't know what he wrote, but if it echoed the words he had placed on the bench's plaque, it'll do just fine.

To the best friend I ever had – thank you.

When Stephanie's twin sister died, she was understandably devastated. Steph – as she liked to be called – and her sister, Lorraine, had just celebrated their twenty-fourth birthdays, an all-singing, all-dancing affair, as you might imagine. Indeed 'dancing', in one way or another, figured highly. Steph and Lorraine were both dancers – Steph in musical theatre and Lorraine in ballet. Steph described herself as a 'jobbing dancer', and while she had fun and enough work to keep her going, she'd never contemplated dancing as a long-term career. For Lorraine, however, it was different. She was on the way to good things, and her prospects, everyone said, were very bright. Opportunities beckoned.

All that came to an end when Lorraine was tragically killed in a multiple pile-up on the Continent. I don't need to explore here how horrendous that was for everyone who knew and loved this wonderful young woman, though it doesn't take much to imagine the horror of it all. And as for Steph as she faced the trauma of the death of her twin sister? We can try to imagine, but we will never know, what it was like for her.

In the early weeks and months of her loss, Steph could hardly speak about how she felt. Articulating her longings was hard, and at times impossible. Thankfully, she had good support – caring friends, a terrific boyfriend, her university counselling service, her priest. She also made contact with me through the Acorns bereavement support service. I've never met Steph and she's never come to one of our groups, but what 'clicked' from an early stage was her sending me emails. And there were times when there were *lots* of them. The best of them were clearly thought out, with questions and statements in a logical sequence. But many of them were nothing more or less than a stream of consciousness. At the start, I tried to respond to her emails right away, dealing with every point and attempting to answer every question. But over time I began to realise that it wasn't my *response* that mattered or any expressions of continued concern, it was simply that, through sending these emails, she had a facility, a reason, a focus for writing things down. I remember once referring in an email to something she'd written to me a number of months before. 'I don't remember writing that,' she replied. 'I have no recollection of it whatsoever.'

Whatever the writing had done – for that issue specifically, or for her welfare in general – 'putting it down', giving it expression, being honest about it had achieved its purpose. Her 'longings' had been articulated, and that was enough. Answers didn't matter. But raising the issues and expressing her longings certainly did.

Lorraine died nine years ago. While I was writing this chapter, I got another email from Steph, the first one in a while. She's married now, and she was sharing the news that she's pregnant with her second child. She's got a little boy already, and she shared thoughts with me about the prospect of having a little girl, and how she'll keep telling her children about her wonderful twin sister, and how she misses her every single day. I suspect she'd have been crying as she wrote to me, but the message of that communication was clearly that Steph was in a good place.

I've never been a person who has kept a regular journal or diary. I know many people who do and derive great benefit from it. In many ways, my writing – such as my blogging and the preparation for this book – has served the same purpose for me over the years. I can't write without processing things for myself.

There is only one period in my life during which I kept a journal, and the story of its importance at that time may be helpful to relate. In 1989, when I was approaching forty and had been in ministry for sixteen years, I had the opportunity to take a period of sabbatical leave. I chose to go to Washington DC and to immerse myself in the worship, teaching and community of the Church of the Saviour. Under the guidance of the charismatic and legendary pastor Gordon Cosby, and learning from many other remarkable people, I had what I can only describe as a life-changing experience. I had two-and-a-half months on my own, my family coming to join me for the final two weeks of my sabbatical and a four-week additional pulpit-exchange in DC.

Those three months were remarkable. They were traumatic and enlivening, scary and creative, self-searching and clarifying. And, from day one, I wrote things down. I don't know why, I just did it. I was encouraged to continue with this in my personal development journey. It seemed to be a natural thing to do. I filled several hard-back notebooks. I wrote about everything – events, feelings, books, people, more feelings, plans, dreams, mistakes. I wrote every day. I took the journals back home with me. I still have them. But I haven't looked at them since. Why not? Because I don't need to. For one thing, they are private and personal. For another, they are of a time. Writing had done its job for me, and that was enough.

In addition, I wrote to my wife Mary every day, sometimes about the same things, but mostly not. I wrote about what was personal to both of us, and that was important too. She's kept these letters. Does she read them? I suspect she does, from time to time. If I die before her, will they matter? You bet they will, because they will become part of the personal legacy I leave with her.

So, through journal and letter writing, I was able to process what was happening to me, and how important my loving relationship was in the midst of all of that. Looking back – and maybe I didn't even realise it at the time – writing in that way helped me get the best out of this important period of my life.

One of the things I *do* remember writing about and reflecting on a great deal was the issue of facing my mortality. Perhaps it was a 'midlife' crisis (if coming up for forty could be described as 'midlife' nowadays) and maybe it was the encouragement of people like Gordon Cosby to look at the important things of life. I wasn't long bereaved of my mother, and I had three young children. I was feeling vulnerable, and facing mortality was part of that. One aspect of that reflection came from a little song.

May There Always Be Sunshine (Пусть всегда будет солнце!) is a Soviet children's song with music by Arkaday Ostrovsky and lyrics by Lev Oshanin. I first heard it in the late 1960s through my occasional dabbling in university folk clubs. The whole song expresses the yearning for lasting peace by millions of people, young and old. The lyrics tell us that in war there are no winners. For our sake, and especially for our children's sake, we must achieve peace and remove the dark clouds that so easily cover the sun. One English translation of the song offers this:

Bright blue sky, sun up on high
That was the little boy's picture
He drew for you, wrote for you too
Just to make clear what he drew:

May there always be sunshine,
May there always be blue skies,
May there always be Mama,
May there always be me.

My little friend, listen my friend,
Peace is the dream of the people,
Hearts old and young never have done
Singing the song you have sung:

I only learned the middle bit, the little chorus part. In phonetic Russian, it goes like this:

Poost vseg-da boo-dyet sohin-she,
Poost vseg-da boo-dyet neyeh-ba,
Poost vseg-da boo-dyet Mama,
Poost vseg-da boo-doo yah.

The human condition craves peace and harmony, security and permanence, and clearly that's what I had to look at too. I recalled someone saying to me that life was like putting your finger in a pail of water and waggling it around. For a while, the water is disturbed, and ripples and splashes are made. But take the finger out, and within seconds you wouldn't even know it had been there. Is that all that life means? And where am I with all of that?

We would love to live in a world where the sun always shines, the skies are ever blue, and our mother – of course – will always be there. We want to know that everything will be OK – and for ever! But it's rare in the fullness of our lives that we give thought to mortality. We know people don't live for ever. We know, therefore, that we – and everyone else – will have to cope with death and all the struggles in bereavement which that reality brings. In the real world we have to learn to live with instability – for we have no choice – and face transience on a daily basis. But the truth is that the pain of loss is too hard for most of us to bear. Our wish to hold on to the security and permanence we know pushes away the reality of death and, therefore, the pain of loss, simply because it is too awful to experience. We will hide from the certainty of our mortality, as if that would ultimately protect us and prevent it happening. My elderly grandmother was fond of saying, 'Don't talk about death, for it might make it happen quicker.' I suspect what she meant was, 'Don't talk about death, for it'll make me have to face the certainty of it.'

The wife of one of our hospice patients was in deep distress and I was asked to spend time with her to offer whatever comfort and consolation I could. Her husband had been admitted the previous day and was clearly close to the end of his life. So his wife was, understandably, distraught. Of all the things she said to me in our time together, I will never forget this cry of pain and devastation:

'It's just not fair that my husband should be dying at his age. He's been a good man, and he's never had a day's illness in his life.

Never smoked, only drank a little, never had a bad word for anyone. It's just not fair – and even worse at his age.'

'How old is your husband?' I enquired.

'Two months short of his ninetieth birthday,' she replied.

I wanted to say: *Oh, for goodness' sake, woman! Being a good man and keeping well is no protection against the reality of death. He's eighty-nine years old. He's got to die of something ...* But, of course, I didn't. Because what this distressed woman was expressing is what, in reality, is in us all. The pain of loss *is* too hard to bear. So we live in a kind of fantasy world where we will never have to face mortality, ours or anyone else's. And when we *have* to face up to it, it is simply too much.

The 16th-century English soldier, poet and courtier Philip Sydney wrote in a sonnet entitled *Astrophil and Stella* these words:

Biting my truant pen, biting myself for spite,
'Fool,' said my Muse to me; 'look in thy heart and write.'

Of course, we may at times feel foolish as we attempt to articulate our longings, share our emotions or record our innermost private thoughts and feelings. Expressing how we feel about facing our mortality – in the face of a trauma or following a bereavement – is scary indeed! But there is much benefit in looking into our own heart, believing that what is there is important, accepting that our personal response to our grief is absolutely valid, and giving expression to that in writing.

So now I'm going off to check my Facebook status. My friend has recently lost her mother, and she's sharing her thoughts every week with her Facebook friends in a kind of 'blog'. I'm not sure I could or would do that. But it works for her, and that's fine. And I'll leave responding to Steph's email till later. Completing this chapter reminds me that I need to take some time for myself for thinking things through and writing them down. *Thank you, Steph, for reminding me how important that is ...*

Dear, dear …

Dear Jim, I'm lost without you here.
Dear Cath, I just can't cope.
Dear mum, I miss you every day.
Dear dad, I'm losing hope.

Dear sis, I'm living half a life,
Dear bro, I live a lie.
Dear God, my life is hellish now.
Dear life! I'd rather die.

Dear diary, here's my honesty.
Dear journal, this is me!
Dear notebook, filled with random lists.
Dear jotter, here's my plea.

Dear self, my words come tumbling out.
Dear blank, I've said enough.
Dear email, I'll go on and on.
Dear Facebook, here's my stuff.

Dear world, I need to say my piece.
Dear silence, will you hear?
Dear emptiness, I need to speak.
Dear what or who? Oh dear …

11. *Academy of Management Journal*, June 1, 1994, vol.37 no.3 722-723 – http://amj.aom.org/content/37/3/722.short
12. *Personality and Social Psychology Bulletin*, 'Health Benefits of Writing about Life Goals', 2001, http://journals.sagepub.com/doi/abs/10.1177/0146167201277003

Chapter 11

Family matters

When the TV celebrity Davina McCall – presenter with Nicky Campbell of the *Long Lost Family* series on ITV, among other things – was interviewed for a piece in a recent edition of *The Radio Times*, she was asked the usual run-of-the-mill questions about her view from the sofa, what she's currently watching on TV and who has the remote control. When she was asked whether she ever had dinner in front of the TV, she replied that she did so very rarely, saying she preferred it when the family chatted together around the dinner table, and that she liked to talk while eating. I was struck by this, and the fact that through most of the interview she referred to 'we' and not 'I', a clear indication of how important it was to place herself in the context of her family life.

Such a focus could, of course, come from her involvement over the years with the *Long Lost Family* programmes, and how deeply she and her co-presenter are affected by mothers being reunited with children given up for adoption, siblings meeting together after being separated for decades, people discovering family members they never knew they had, and many other emotional reunions. How could you not be moved by playing a part in facilitating such moments of healing, reconciliation and love in a family? But what came over in the brief *Radio Times* interview was that the importance of family isn't just due to her work; it is something that is an integral part of her and how she sees herself in the world. In short, for Davina McColl, it's clear that family matters, and matters a great deal.

Most of the bereavements that affect us happen within families. Friends die too, of course, and the effect on us of the death of someone who is often closer and more important to us than any family member can't be over-estimated. We are touched, too, by the deaths of people in our social circle, church, street, neighbour-hood, workplace ... for there also is a 'community' aspect to loss, where we are all affected by the death of someone important, even though we weren't particularly close to them personally.

John Donne, in his often-quoted poem *No Man is an Island* writes:

> *Every man is a piece of the continent,*
> *A part of the main.*
> *If a clod be washed away by the sea,*
> *Europe is the less.*
> *As well as if a promontory were.*
> *As well as if a manor of thy friend's*
> *Or of thine own were:*
> *Any man's death diminishes me,*
> *Because I am involved in mankind ...*

If we can cope with the parochialism of the 'Europe' reference or the gender-specific language of its time, we know that Donne is communicating an important truth. So the death of someone we have never met can have its impact, for the loss from our lives of someone we admire, a role model, a 'hero' figure, someone in the public eye who is important to us, irrevocably changes the world around us. But most of the deaths we experience will be within our own family circle, and such bereavements will hit us hard – because family matters.

We talk, therefore, about 'a grieving family' or 'a family in mourning', and that of course is quite correct. For if each family is an important building block of our society, and that family is destabilised by a death, society sees it primarily as a family issue. Of course, we know that individuals are involved – a husband grieving the loss of his wife; parents struggling with the death of a child; the death of a parent, a sibling, a grandparent, an uncle or aunt. The list goes on, affecting individuals in the ever-widening circles of every family. But when viewed from the out-side – the family sitting in the front three rows in church for a funeral; the other mourners waiting at the crematorium for the family limousines to arrive; the immediate family members taking the cords for the lowering of the coffin into a grave; 'the chief mourners' shaking hands with others at the graveside – then we see a *family* in grief, a family unit coping with loss.

That's fine, of course, because when Tom Gordon dies, the Gordon family – in all its branches and connections – will be in mourning. That's a given. A family will be blanketed by grief.

But it is *within* that context of family that I want in this chapter to look at bereavement issues, challenge some assumptions and point to some aspects of grief and loss which need to be considered.

A family in mourning does not grieve – as a participant in one of our bereavement programmes affirmed so clearly – in 'one homogeneous lump'. Within any family dealing with a death there will be many different people reacting in very different ways, and it's here that some problems arise.

In the best of families, the love, openness, respect and support which are fundamental to how that family functions can mitigate against good support in bereavement, because of what I've come to refer to as the 'conspiracy of silence'. Let me offer a simple example. Len's mother had died. It wasn't a 'difficult' death, although Len, as an only son, missed her deeply. Though married and living in Edinburgh – a long way from the family home in

Brighton – Len was in touch with his parents regularly, by phone, Facetime and email.

When his mother died, Len spent some weeks with his father sorting through 'mum's stuff' and getting 'all the affairs in order'. And, in time, it was back to Edinburgh and regular communication back and forward from a distance. 'Whether it was a phonecall or a Facetime,' Len told me, 'conversations always began more or less in the same way.'

'How are you, dad?'

'OK, son. And how are you?'

'Not too bad at all.'

'What do you make of the Brexit developments?'

'Which ones do you mean?'

'Oh, you know, what the Prime Minister was going on about after the Brussels shenanigans at the weekend …'

'And the chat would continue, about Brexit and the US presidency, Westminster and Holyrood politics, *Newsnight* and *The Andrew Marr Show*. And when we'd exhausted that, it would be what was worth watching on TV, and "Storm Hilda" coming in from the Atlantic, and how my kids were doing at school. All the time I was thinking about mum. I knew dad was too. But it was too hard for him to say so. And I knew he was concerned about me. But it was too hard for him to ask. And me? I couldn't find a way of broaching the subject either, without feeling it would be making things ten times worse for him and make us both sad again. There was an "elephant in the room" that both of us were doing our best to pretend wasn't there.'

Common? Indeed, it is – and I know so from my own family experience, as I have described in an earlier chapter. Normal? That too, for this 'silence' issue is predicated on respect, being more concerned about the feelings and welfare of someone you love than you are about yourself.

Len said to me once: 'If I was to be honest with my dad and tell him how I was *really* struggling, it would have become about me and not him, and my sorrow would have given him an additional burden to carry that he didn't need, because he had enough sorrow to deal with of his own. And if I'd forced the issue and got him to talk about aspects of his life he wasn't able or willing to talk about, it would have caused a problem for both of us.'

Just as with my own father, Len loved his dad and didn't want to make things worse for him by unburdening himself honestly. And his dad was doing the same. So they'd slipped into the 'How are you?' / 'I'm fine, and how are you?' scenario, never acknowledging their sadness.

But what did this achieve? Increased isolation for Len and for his dad, perhaps? ... Processing the loss alone? ... Feeling more remote? If so, then that sense of remoteness *could* have created a barrier and separation between a father and son at the very time they needed to face the future together. Thankfully, in the case of Len and his dad, that never happened. But it could easily have done.

There is also the issue within families of what I could call the 'compare and contrast' approach to grief. When my friend's dad died – a wise, respected and much-loved senior figure in a big family – the whole family was in mourning. My friend's smaller family unit was in mourning too, of course, as a branch of the whole, but it was the grieving process within that smaller unit that impacted on her. 'My husband and I talked, of course,' she told me, 'as we've always done. We'd had other deaths to deal with before – my mum, his parents, aunts and uncles, and the like. But we were conscious that this was the first major bereavement our kids were experiencing.' Her children – aged ten, twelve and fourteen – were having to process the death of someone they loved for the first time.

'I was fascinated,' my friend said, 'by their immediate reaction to Papa's death. Maria, the youngest, just prattled, because that's what she does, non-stop, "motor-mouth", on and on and on. Denise, the twelve-year-old, went straight to her bedroom and put on loud music. I told her to put her earphones on because the house was rocking with the noise. But I could still hear the infernal racket leaking into the ether. And Jamie? Well he just sat in the corner and said nothing. Just watched and listened. Took it all in, I reckoned – and I know that, because he was able to quote stuff back at us much later. But he just fell into silence, because that's his way.'

Three young people, all of whom had a loving relationship with their grandfather, and who were processing their sorrow in very different ways, and all – as my friend confided in me – out of their own personalities. Did she compare one with the other? Of course she did, for that's where her interest lay, as did her concern as a mother. But did she say that one was right and another wrong, that this way was appropriate and that way wasn't? Not at all. Because to have done so would have been a judgement – and that's not what three children needed from their mum in their sorrow.

We're all different. Families *can't* grieve as a 'homogeneous lump'. Within each family unit there will be variations, just as the individual family members are distinctive in so many other ways. So why should the style in which we process our bereavements be any exception? Yet there *are* times when comparisons of the different ways people grieve can lead to judgements, criticisms and tensions.

Take the obvious contrast between a dramatic outpouring of grief and a quiet, dignified, almost stoical approach. Neither is right or wrong. Both are appropriate – and I've seen enough of the spectrum of reactions to death within families over many years to know the truth of that. But within the family unit itself, such comparisons can cause problems. From, 'For goodness' sake, woman, pull yourself together. This is not the time or the place ...'

through, 'He's not cried yet. It's a worry, because he still hasn't cracked ...' or even, 'She couldn't have loved him as much, or her grief would be much worse than it is ...'

My way need not be your way. And his way need not be her way. Comparisons are OK. It's what we see and know, and we can't stop ourselves. But judgements, criticisms and tensions are unhelpful, for they might drive wedges between people just when healing and togetherness is needed, and it might force people into a deeper isolation in loss because nobody appears to understand.

All the bereavement research tells us that there are categories of people who are at greater 'risk' in bereavement than others. There are those, for example, who have had to deal with a sudden or violent death or even suicide. There are people who have no body to lay to rest, when there is a loss at sea for example. Several deaths close together can be a factor. A young death brings its own trauma. There is also the category of 'dysfunctionality', where a family already lives with fractured relationships and poor communication. In such a context, tensions already exist which are, not surprisingly, increased by the stresses and strains of a death. Such 'risk factors' have to be carefully monitored, for if people are unable to process their loss in a non-judgemental atmosphere of mutual respect, they may need additional help and support in their bereavement from outwith the family circle.

Another area of difficulty within families is the 'Who does what?' issue, and the additional stress of an appropriate 'When' for such things.

One session in our bereavement programmes is devoted to the fraught area of 'business-type' affairs which can be a heavy burden for people to carry in their bereavement. James McDonald, a financial outreach worker with a local Citizens Advice Bureau, is our current resource person for that topic, and the issues explored range far and wide – from power of attorney to wills, from council tax to benefits, from HMRC to utility companies, from banks to broadband providers. There are specifics, of course, about which people need guidance. But there are three threads that run through all our discussions. The first is how much there is to do following any death. The second is how hard it is to concentrate on all of these things and do them justice when your 'head isn't in the right place'. And the third is the cry from the heart: 'And I'm having to do it all by myself.'

The important thing, therefore, is to be willing to ask for help with some or all of these things. But that's hard, sometimes, when people feel they are 'put upon', or that they *should* be able to cope as they've always done. They may experience a sense of failure when they don't feel motivated to deal with things or don't have the clarity of thought to tackle them in the right way. Is there an appropriate time to scatter a loved-one's ashes, and where might it best be done? When is the right time to deal with the belongings – clothes, and the like – of a person who has died?

Stu was a man in his fifties who had to deal with the death of his father. The old man had lived with Stu's sister – widowed herself – for several years, and the family unit worked well in an open, supportive and sensitive fashion. Stu's dad had died following a fall, a resulting pneumonia and a short spell in hospital. He was eighty-nine. Stu lived a long way away, and though he and his sister made all the arrangements for the funeral over the phone in a respectful and mutually supportive way, Stu couldn't go 'down south' till a few days before the funeral. He was surprised to find when he arrived that his sister had already cleared out all of her father's clothes and many of his personal things. 'Thank God there were a few bits and pieces I could look through and choose which ones to keep,' Stu told me. 'But I felt that my father had been thrown away with his things, before I'd really had a chance to say goodbye.' For Stu it was too soon. For his sister it was necessary.

Both were right, but the course of action his sister had chosen took no cognisance of the fact that there was another approach that was equally valid.

One of the things we encourage, therefore, is for people to express their own feelings, anxieties and approaches, even though they may be at odds with the views of other members of their family. Often – as Stu did, for example – people take the opportunity to 'tell it as it is' in the safety of working with us and other bereaved people, when that hasn't been possible for them in the respectfulness of the family unit.

One widow told us that she'd asked her daughter if she'd like to come to a bereavement programme with her. The daughter declined. At first the woman thought her daughter was either ducking the issues or not being supportive of her mother. But as time went on and her confidence in sharing her own feelings and aspects of her loss grew, she realised that her daughter had given her space and time, and a forum in which she could be herself without wondering what her daughter was going to think about what she was saying.

What people need in bereavement is patience and time. With the best will in the world, even in the best of families, people feel that neither patience nor time is really available to them. They feel constrained to act the part they perceive is the right one for the peace and unity of the family. And sometimes that means they can't be truly honest with themselves or others. So it's not disloyal and unnatural to find a forum or a person outside the family unit with whom to share their feelings. It might just be what people need to cope with and make sense of what is going on.

When I was a parish minister, I conducted the funeral of one of my favourite church members, Barry, a craggy old man who for the latter years of his life had been struggling with Parkinson's Disease. His wife, Bella, was devoted to him, and though she was a fair age herself, gave herself self-sacrificially to his care. I visited them both regularly, and whatever benefit that was to them, I always came away enriched by my time with two wonderful people. It was sad when Barry died. It was a relief too, of course, but we were all conscious of how vulnerable Bella would be, and many in the church were committed to offering her support in her bereavement.

As it turned out, I was on a two-week holiday after Barry's funeral, so, apart from visiting Bella before I left, it was almost a month after Barry's death that I called to see her again. I was surprised to find a 'For Sale' board in the garden of her home. There was no reply when I rang the doorbell.

After I'd made enquiries, I discovered that just under two weeks after the funeral the family had informed her that she was moving into sheltered housing – at the beginning of the following week. I found out where she was and went to see her right away. I found her in a lovely, new, cosy, well-appointed two-bedroom flat in a development on the other side of the town. I spent an hour with her in tears – both of us. 'It's too soon,' she told me. 'I never got time to say goodbye to sixty years of memories.'

'Family matters', and of course that is true. A family unit is, and should always be, the primary unit of support and security following a death. But there may be times – outlined in the stories above – when we need to reach beyond our families for the necessary, honest and open support we crave, so that we can return to the care of our family unit more able to support our loved ones.

I conclude this chapter with a personal reflection. One of the most difficult things a widow or widower has to face is the 'empty home' syndrome. There is always the issue of going home to be alone, putting the key in the door and knowing there's no one there to welcome you, spending time by yourself when you've had the constant companionship of a life-partner for many years.

All the support, concern and opportunities in the world cannot and will not protect a bereaved person from that pain. Some cope with it better than others, of course. For many, the home is a place of safety and peace, where they are surrounded by many happy memories; for others, it's a place of torture, where the oppressive 'aloneness' crowds in on them all the time. For many, there are opportunities to adjust, change a routine, alter the surroundings, make choices that weren't possible before; for others, there's the pain of sleeping in an empty bed, waking up in an empty room, experiencing the emptiness of no casual conversation. After talking with several recently-bereaved widows and widowers over a number of months, I tried to capture their feelings and reflections in one place. This is how it turned out:

Home alone without you; on my own again;
one more empty evening, never knowing when
home alone without you will turn out OK.
Home alone without you – every day.

Home alone's a daily thing I have to face.
Minutes drag like hours; hours seem like days.
Home alone still often catches me off guard.
Home alone without you – always hard.

Home alone without you … I don't have the choice –
ages spent in silence listening for your voice;
home alone embraced by emptiness and pain.
Home alone without you – once again.

Home alone – becoming all too commonplace.
How I long to hold you; see your smiling face!
Home alone's a trial! I'm not coping well.
Home alone without you – this is hell!

Home alone with memories … that'll have to do;
all those hours remembering being close to you.
Home alone without you will turn out OK.
Home alone – still with you every day.

However it's expressed, this is one issue a family will not be able to deal with, no matter how hard they try. Bella's family moved her to a new home with the assumption, presumably, that they were helping her deal with her loss. And in one way they were, because they knew she was safe. But I can't help thinking it was more for their benefit than hers, for, no matter what, Bella was still going have to deal with being alone without Barry. It was a process and a pain she had to face – and no one could do it but her.

By way of contrast, Nico, an elderly widower from a big Italian family, said to me once, 'I've got more dishes of home-made lasagne in my freezer than I'll even be able to look at, and my phone's red hot at all hours with the girls wondering how I am, and can they come over, and am I eating, and did I call the plumber, and what am I planning for Christmas. *Mamma mia!* I just want to be left alone, sometimes, to be sad …'

'Family matters.' Nico knew that, and he knew that he mattered to his family, as he'd always done and always would. But a family that smothered, cushioned, tried too hard? He didn't really need that – any more than he needed another dish of home-made lasagne!

Getting there?

Two steps forward, one step back;
Ups and downs; a jibe, a tack;
Ins and outs; swing high, swing low.
What journey's this I'm on?
Veering left, and then diving right;
Clear as day, then out of sight;
Here and there, then to and fro …
What am I set upon?

Quick, quick, slow, then slower still;
Hard to climb, but fast downhill;
Near the top, then more to go …
When will it all be done?
Rising high, then crash and burn;
Open roads, then dangerous turns;
Fearsome tides; going with the flow …
When will my race be run?

Straight and true, and tortuous bends;
Miles and miles that never end.
Wheels that turn, but nothing goes …
What have I taken on?
Far to go, and further yet;
Snail's pace, then it's *Exocet*!
Good and bad; more highs and lows …
Where's my direction gone?

Straight and true, then round about;
Silent pain; in with a shout;

Fast and loose; an awful time ...
Why is this so unfair?
Backwards? Forwards? Where to go?
Upwards? Downwards? I don't know ...
Seas to conquer? Hills to climb?
I'm getting there ... but where?

Chapter 12

Newfoundland, and not New York

As I hope has been apparent throughout this book, the use of metaphors in working with bereaved people is extremely useful. If there's a visual image which can be utilised to explain a tricky concept, or a picture that can illustrate a complicated idea or hard-to-express feelings, everyone benefits. All the images in the preceding chapters have been used beneficially with many of the bereaved people I've worked with over the years. My son – also a writer and poet – has said to me often enough that I speak in metaphors. I'm not unhappy with that. But perhaps the most enlightening times are when a metaphor is offered as a way of conceptualising an idea, and is then taken on by other people, pushed this way and that, added to and elaborated on, so that it becomes even more useful to them in a personal way. When people take a metaphor and use it as their own, interesting things happen.

I have written before about the pressure people experience in the early stages of loss as they try to make sense of the new and confusing feelings which bereavement has created in them. What people need at that point more than anything else is to be listened to – discussed in the opening chapter of this book. This is not to say they have a problem or are reacting in an unnatural or unhealthy way. It's simply that people don't know how to make sense of what's happening to them, and therefore have little understanding of what's normal and what isn't. And, as also explored earlier, there may be few – if any – opportunities for them to 'check out' their feelings in a society which is more 'closed down' than we think it is.

The bereavement programmes which I've scoped out and developed last for six sessions, a length of time that has shown itself to work and to do all that we set out to achieve. The programmes continue to evaluate well, so we stick with what we know and what we trust.

The final week takes the form of a kind of review – looking at what's been gained from the programme; touching on things that may have been missed; and looking to what the future might hold. It's often in this final session that people find they have the confidence to articulate issues for themselves and put into words their deepest and most important thoughts and ideas.

Orla, widowed after forty-four years of marriage, put it like this – unprompted, I should say:

> *I feel I've been thrown a lifeline and, though I was floundering in a big ocean, I've managed to grab hold of it and find that I've been hauled into a boat. I'm still scared. But at least now I know that there are other people in the boat too, and there's a kind of safety in being together. I can get my breath back. I know I'm still alive, and I thank God for that. I'm in a boat, still bobbing about, not really knowing what's going to happen next or how we'll manage. But at least we're alive and in a boat, and that's just about OK for now.*

It was a lovely moment. Orla's sentiment, beautifully illustrated with the image of the boat, evoked nods and appreciative comments from the others in the group. They recognised, right away, the truth of what she was saying. She'd articulated what many were thinking. She'd created a metaphor with which others could identify.

At this point, I would usually try to offer my own thanks for her articulation of an important idea and affirm the worth of the image she'd offered us. But I didn't have the chance. For, before

I'd found the words, one of the other members of the group – Vince, a man of similar age and circumstances – took the metaphor further and made it personal to himself. In animated fashion and with a big smile, he said:

> *Ah, you're right, Orla. The truth is it's my* Titanic *that's gone down – and yours too. The journey I've been on is over. The bloody iceberg of the death of my wife has seen to that. But there's hope, isn't there? I'm in the boat with you. It looks like there's the possibility of being safe after all.*

Vince paused. We thought he was finished. If he had been, it would have been a useful enough contribution of itself. But he wasn't. Instead he said, gently but firmly:

> *And, you know, when we get to shore again – and I'm quite sure we will – it won't be the shore we set out to get to. It'll be a different shore, a strange new country we've never seen before and know nothing about. Instead of being in New York we'll be in Newfoundland. And that'll just have to be where the new part of our life will begin.*

If we could have bottled the moment and used it in every bereavement programme from then on it would have been wonderful. Because Vince was right. And everyone else knew he was right. He'd made the metaphor his own. He'd put his own construct on it. He'd made his own use of the articulation of another group member. And now *he* had a visual image – and an articulation he could share with others in the future – which he would never forget.

Bereavement support in any form, in a one-to-one relationship or in a group-based process, over a six-week block or monthly over a year or more, in informal drop-in circumstances or in professionally therapeutic environments, should of course never be offered with 'rescuing' in mind. People who are bereaved must deal with their bereavement and work it through and not have it covered or masked by the well-meaning care and compassion of others. Of course, people will *ask* to be rescued at times and cry out for help – 'Can't you take the pain away?' – because grief is hard to bear. But a rescuing approach only serves to deflect things for a time, for each individual will eventually have to deal with the reality and the struggle of loss. But there is no denying – nor should there be – that when good care and compassion are offered and bereaved people, as a result, feel less alone and stronger in their ability to cope, they have a greater sense of safety.

To draw from Orla's image: to allow people to feel they can take a breath; to give them the opportunity to normalise their experiences and feelings; to create an environment where they know they are not alone, even though they may still be scared and uncertain of their future … brings untold benefit. This is fundamental to all the bereavement work we do.

But it was the *next* stage of the metaphor which allowed *me* to find expression of another issue which is so common in loss – and that's the 'Newfoundland and not New York' part. Here you had Vince telling us he understood for himself what the death of his wife had left him with. He wasn't going to drown when his *Titanic* had gone down. He had the capacity – from his own resolve; from strong religious practices; from open and positive support of family and friends; and, thankfully, from the life-raft he'd been on with us for the six weeks of our programme – to cope, to face the future. But Vince knew well enough that this future was completely unknown. He'd been heading happily to New York with his wife by his side. But now, after the trauma of his ship being sunk by the 'bloody iceberg', he'd landed on the unknown shore.

This was his Newfoundland. He'd make the best of it, of course, happy as he was to be safe and have a new beginning. But he knew nothing of the language or the customs of this strange land. He had no grasp of the road system nor the history of the place. He had no clue what dangers he would face or what issues he'd have to resolve. It was new, and strange, and different, and not a little scary.

The Unknown Shore is a novel published in 1959 by Patrick O'Brian. It's the story of two friends, Jack Byron and Tobias Barrow, who sail aboard the HMS Wager as part of a round-the-world voyage in 1740. The expedition is beset by storms while rounding Cape Horn and the Wager is shipwrecked on an island off the coast of Chile. Some of the crew reject the authority of their officers and leave the captain, some officers and the remainder of the crew on the island when they sail away in a boat built from the wreck. The marooned officers make their way to a Spanish settlement with the help of the native people.

This was not what the crew of the ship, officers or men, either wanted or expected. The storms of the journey forced them to change course. The violence of these storms wrecked them on an unknown shore. And as if that wasn't trauma enough, officers and crew now had to make sense of life in this strange place, with all the tensions, uncertainties, pain and confusion that resulted. If we could have put Vince in that drama, it would have been all too familiar to him. Indeed, he could probably have written the screenplay all by himself.

In the world of gaming (known better to my grandsons than to me, I have to confess), in the *Fable III* series of action role-playing video games, the Unknown Shore is the first destination reached by the Hero and Walter after their ship is destroyed on the voyage to Aurora. The region contains two treasure chests, one on the beach to the left of the shipwreck and one near the top of the steps above the portal sealing the entrance to Shadelight. Once you enter Shadelight, you will never be able to return to this region again.

Here is a different take on an unknown destination, for as with most gaming explorations, it isn't where you *are* that matters, it is how you move on from there, how you attain the next level or go through the next portal. There will be dangers – and failures – but there may also be trophies, successes and, indeed, treasure-chests to gain along the way.

Such is the way of things with loss. Our journey on the oceans of life is seldom trouble-free. Most of the storms we face we will ride out. But there will be times when we are shipwrecked by our traumas, thrown with the Wager onto an unknown shore. In that new and strange place, tensions will rise, fears will accumulate, mistakes will be made and failures will be experienced. But for many, despite all of that – and even though you never get to your Aurora – there might yet be treasure-chests to find and new portals to explore.

For Orla and Vince, it was the uncertainties caused by the death of a life-partner that had thrown them up onto this new shoreline. I have no idea what that is like for them. I still have my wife with me and I know the journey we're on and something of the destinations we hope to reach. But I remember very well the unknown shore I was cast upon when my aunt died.

My father was one of eight children. 'Three boys then a girl, followed by three boys then a girl' had been the Gordon family mantra for many years. My father's death left only one of his siblings, the youngest of the eight, for whom – following her husband's death – I was designated as next-of-kin. In time, I had power of attorney for her and, during the final years of her life following a stroke, organised her nursing home care, dealt with all her business affairs, and looked after her with all the love and attention she deserved.

I loved my aunt Kit, and she loved me. Our journey together was a good one. We had no idea where it would take us. But we were happy with the sharing, the direction of travel, and the safety of our relationship. I was devastated when she died. I was prepared for it (in my head, at least). After all, she was eighty-five and in failing health. We hadn't missed anything – what had needed to be done and said had been done and said. Everything was in order – business, relationships, emotions. We were 'sorted'. But her death threw me onto another strange and unknown coastline. It was the land where not one of my father's siblings was left. It was a country where I became one of the senior generation of the Gordons. It was the alien environment of being expected, I suppose, to be the depository of family wisdom, and stories, and traditions, and who knows what. It's a land I've now learned to enjoy. But at the start? There was no prospect of enjoyment at all.

As I mentioned in an earlier chapter, Chris Jones, widowed for ten years now, comes to a session of our bereavement programmes and shares his own story of his journey of loss. Sometimes he talks about his recent decision to move house, to a place which is better laid out for him on his own, and one in which he can engage with family and friends in a different way. 'To be honest,' he tells us, 'the old house was like a favourite coat that didn't fit any more. I *tried* to make it fit, for after all it was the best coat I had. But over the years I realised it wasn't going to work. So I decided to change coats. It was scary, because I wasn't sure what coat I needed or how it would work. But it had to be done. And now I feel safe and secure in my new surroundings.'

Using this different image, Chris is articulating the 'safety' issue. What was familiar had gone. He had to accept that over time. Accepting a new beginning – and it took time to realise it – was the starting point to a different, though scary, future life.

Orla and Vince had it right. Loss is as devastating as the sinking of the *Titanic*. The hopes and dreams, the excitement of the journey and the expectations of reaching your 'New York' destination give you all the pleasure you feel you'll ever need. But the sinking has taken all of that away. And that's a very scary place to be. There are lifelines that you can grab and rescue boats that appear. You can feel safe again – scared but safe; fearful but not alone; unprepared but relieved; angry but grateful – with all the jumble and juxtaposition of emotions the aftermath of the trauma brings. Life can begin again after a trauma – thank God.

But where? On a shoreline not of your choosing; in Newfoundland and not New York; where there are no familiar landmarks; when hopes and dreams have been superseded by the unknown and the uncertain. You are where you are, not where you'd like to be. But you have survived – and what's to do but to pull your boat up onto the shore, sit down and take stock, find a new resolve and begin to explore a new land after loss.

Where?

Where am I now,
this new and unfamiliar place
of loss and grief,
of fear and doubt,
of strange bewilderment
where I've been cast
now time has done its worst?

Where is this shore,
this alien, unknown, foreign land
of sights and sounds,
of sense and scent,
of weird confusion,
where I've arrived,
unwelcomed and unsure?

Where are my dreams,
those hopes and plans worked out with you,
of life and love,
of journeys shared,
companions on the way.
What does life mean
when all of that has gone?

Where do I go
when pathways are not clear to me,
so when I turn
and try to move
I can't, and feel so lost?
Where might I go
when everything feels wrong?

When will I know
that this is where I must begin
to make the best
of who I am?
When can I say, *It's now*
I'll make a start
exploring where I am, and why?

When will I find
new purpose in this different place?
Will life and love
make sense again?
Will hope return to me?
It's hard to wait
till I can leave my altered shore ...

Chapter 13

Hope,
hope to the last!

In his remarkable book *A Grief Observed*, C S Lewis reflects power-fully and movingly on the death of his wife, Joy. He talks about instability, not in the sense of not coping, but because nothing seemed to stay the same for long. Just as he was emerging from one phase and felt he was moving on, it all happened over again and it was like he'd gone back to the start. Was this going round in a circle or being on a spiral? If the latter, did that indicate he was going up or down? He struggles with the 'How long?' question, as we all do with loss. But, most meaningfully and honestly for me, he touches on the awful experiencing of the vast emptiness of his bereavement again and again, each time the effect of his loss being as powerful as it was the very first time. It was, he says, like having the same leg cut off again and again and again.

This is another expression of Dr Mike Wilson's tide going in and out. Sometimes we feel in control and at other times we are overwhelmed when the waves come back and wet our feet. *It always recurs.*

This is Chris Jones recognising that he is forced to find a 'new normal' as life adjusts, often painfully and slowly, to a new way of living without a loved one. *Nothing stays put.*

This is Kellie Anderson understanding that this adjustment has consequences, on the body as well as the emotions, on the mind as well as the soul. We become, essentially, different people in bereavement, and sometimes we don't know who we are and how to take care of ourselves. *Am I going up or down?*

This is James McDonald helping us deal with the myriad of things which threaten to overwhelm us in bereavement, things that demand focus, motivation, clarity of thought, when we are cast down by tiredness and can't concentrate as we once did. *Round and round … Am I going in circles?*

This is, in short, the reality of loss.

Within all of that, we know for ourselves that C S Lewis is right when he asks:

> *How often – will it be for always? – how often will the vast emptiness astonish me like a complete novelty and make me say, 'I never realised my loss till this moment'?*

We know that other people are bereaved. We have seen them, talked with them, supported them. But we do not, and we cannot, fully understand what is happening to them. We can never say with any certainty whatsoever: 'I know how you feel.' So when we ourselves are bereaved, the feelings we experience are new, and different, and very strange. We are forced to inhabit an alien world with no signposts to reassure us we are on the right road.

Loss is intrinsically personal. There's no right or wrong way to feel. You might be in C S Lewis' 'spiral' and you might be going 'up', but you don't know that or how far there is to go. You might be going 'down' and you don't know how far you still have to fall. You might feel lots of emotions at once or experience a bad day after you've had a good one.

I suggested to a widow once that she might be having good days and bad days. 'No,' she replied firmly, 'I have *days* and bad days. I have no good days yet.' So, having learned from this encounter, I suggested to a young man whose mother had died have he might have days when he felt bad about things and days when he felt better. 'Days?' he responded. 'There are *hours,* minutes even … chunks of days of varying lengths, when I'm up and down, coping and tearful, feeling good and feeling awful.'

In preceding chapters we have explored a number of these issues and why they arise. Strong feelings often come out of the blue, triggered by music, memories, a sense of place, a mood, a smell, what people say. There will be times of acceptance and times of pain, times of adjustment and times of yearning. We'll feel shock and numbness; there will be lots of tears; we may feel worn out, even exhausted; there will be intense feelings of anger and guilt; we might lose motivation or not be able to concentrate as we'd like to. All of this is normal, perfectly normal. We're not going mad! The people whose stories are told in this book give voice to that. And through their stories you might just feel less alone and isolated in your grief.

Lots of people feel guilty about their anger, but it's OK to express strong feelings. We are human, after all. So why shouldn't we be angry and give vent to our cries of suffering? Which of us hasn't asked, 'Why, oh why, is this happening to me?'

Talking and being listened to will help. You needn't go through this by yourself. There are plenty of good people and agencies out there willing and able to help. Don't be afraid to talk about the person who has died. People in your life might not mention their name because they don't want to upset you. But if *you* feel you can't talk to them, it can make you feel isolated.

William Shakespeare, in *Macbeth,* has Malcolm say this to Macduff:

Merciful heaven!
What, man! Ne'er pull your hat upon your brows.
Give sorrow words. The grief that does not speak
Whispers the o'erfraught heart and bids it break.

Give sorrow words. What hat might we be pulling over our heads, I wonder, to prevent us speaking of our sorrow and being honest about our grief? We are unique human beings. Our relationship with the person who has died is unique. And so our bereavement will be unique.

There is no set length of time. There is no end-point to grief. There is adjustment, of course, and a growth in confidence and ability to cope. Bad days may be further apart. And, in time, good days – even the ability to laugh again – will emerge from the days where we simply feel we're just functioning.

Helen Keller, an American author, political activist and lecturer, was the first deaf-blind person to earn a Bachelor of Arts degree. Outspoken in her convictions, she campaigned for women's suffrage and the rights of working people, and spoke out against unjust wars. In her book, *We Bereaved*[13], she says this:

> *I have received many letters from people stricken with grief, and I have always felt poignantly my helplessness before their sorrow. My heart yearns to speak the word that would soothe their anguish, but how futile are words in the ears of those who mourn. I can only take their hands in mine and pray that the love and sympathy in my heart may over-flow into theirs. I too have loved and lost. I too must often fight hard to keep a steadfast faith.*

Wonderful stuff! But it is this quotation I want to spend a little more time on.

> *We bereaved are not alone. We belong to the largest company in all the world – the company of those who have known suffering.*

'Fine!' you say. 'But I *feel* alone … I know others have been and are, even now, bereaved. I know people die, and since the beginning of time people have had to deal with loss. But it is no use to me *whatsoever* for you to tell me others are also bereaved when I feel that no one could possibly have experienced what I'm going through now.'

I get that, of course. But I don't offer Helen Keller's quote to dismiss the pain and isolation of our loss. I offer it as an affirmation of hope.

What Helen Keller says to me is this: If people have been bereaved in all of history, then what is happening to *us* is not new. And if humanity has had to deal with death through all the ages and has not been wiped out by the reality of it, then we can be sure that the world will survive death. If humanity has survived through the devastation of loss in world wars and the pain of the individual loss of a loved one, might it not be true that we are being given a signal that we too will survive? And is that not an affirmation of hope?

There's an old Irish proverb which tells us that:

Hope is the physician of each misery.

I believe that to be true, and I am grateful that I have seen countless examples of that physician offering the balm of healing in the brokenness and misery of bereavement. That is not to belittle the pain or to dismiss the anguish. It is to affirm that, as others have found, the same hope might also be available to us.

The helpful website *Guideposts*[14], in its section headed 'Stories of hope', offers us this assurance:

Hopeful stories are windows into the wonderful possibilities life has to offer. Stories of hope bring to life the ways in which people support each other; miracles make lives better, and individuals find new roads through challenging times. Turn to stories about hope whenever you need an encouraging boost on your path toward your best life.

So I want to end this chapter and the issues we have explored in this book by offering you three such 'stories of hope' to encourage you, in your bereavement, toward your 'best path of life', whatever that might be or wherever it might take you.

Johnny had been a season ticket holder at Easter Road for more than twenty years, passionate, as his father and grandfather had been before him, in following his beloved Hibs in the Scottish Premier League. He *had* been, but he'd given up going to matches when his wife Felicia had been diagnosed with cancer, and he needed to give his time to her care. For two years it had been a balancing act of work and care, time away from home and precious time – especially at the weekends – with Felicia. When she died and he had choices to make about the use of his time, he couldn't bring himself to go back to Easter Road. 'Why should I enjoy myself?' he would ask. 'What would people think of me, so soon after Felicia's death? And anyway, would I not be disloyal to her if I chose to have fun?'

In time, about eighteen months after Felicia had died, and having succumbed to the persuasion of his friends, he went back to a game. He was nervous, of course, but good friends made it as easy for him as possible. A couple of pints before the game helped too. But the high point was a last-minute winner for Hibs. A scrambled goal … the home crowd on its feet … bear-hugs and handshakes among mates … the Hibs' scorer coming to the stand for the adulation of the crowd. 'And d'you know,' Johnny told me, 'I had tears in my eyes. For a moment I thought they'd done it all just for me. And when the centre-forward waved at the crowd and gave a double thumbs-up, you know, he was looking *right in my direction.*'

Hope for Johnny, crystallised in a beautiful moment of unrestrained pleasure, and all for him and him alone.

It's not too much to say it was a turning point for him. It wasn't a magic wand that made it all instantly better, and in truth he went home after that first venture back at the football consumed with guilt that he'd had such a great time. But it was a start. It was a glimpse of hope, and thankfully he recognised that. In a couple of months, he'd renewed his season ticket for the following season. He was looking forward to a few more late winners, and even Hibs winning the Premier League. Well, there's always hope, isn't there?

For Thelma, the decision centred around an invitation to a party. Widowed after fifty-seven years of marriage, she had coped with bereavement with dignity, calmness, self-knowledge and sound common sense. In any measurement – hers and others' – she had done well. But the struggle for Thelma was going to 'functions' on her own. Attending church was just about manageable, though there were some wobbly moments there too. But going to orchestral concerts, attending meetings of the local Historical Society, participating in outings with the Rotary and Inner Wheel were all avoided. People understood, of course, and no one put Thelma under any pressure. She was happy enough to spend time by herself, embraced by happy memories of her husband.

The crunch came, however, a year or so after her husband's death, when she was invited to her neighbour's eightieth birthday party. She'd had the same neighbours for forty years and, under-standably, had leaned on them for a lot of support in the first year of her bereavement. They had been all she could have expected them to be. But what was Thelma to do? The party was to be at the local golf club where her husband had once been Club Captain. It was all she had been avoiding for a year or more. But could she avoid this one?

In the end, she decided to go. This all took place before I knew Thelma, so I wasn't privy to the thought processes that led to her decision or the agonies she would have gone through before, during and, perhaps, after the party – though I could well imagine. But when she told me her story some months later, I remember her saying this: 'I knew it was going to be hard, but on balance I decided the right thing to do was to go. There are a lot of "shoulds" in bereavement, and that just creates pressure. So I'd learned early on to replace each "should" with a "could". Because that's a permission word, and it gave me choices. So the invitation wasn't a "should" for me. But it was a "could". I had a choice. So I chose to go to the party. But I knew I had to have a strategy. I decided to set myself a time-limit, so that I knew it would be OK to "take my leave" when I'd done my bit. I kept an eye on the club-room clock. In the end, I stayed much longer than I thought I would. But the strategy helped me anyway. And it turned out much better than I had expected.'

Thelma still doesn't go out much on her own. She 'could', of course, but she chooses not to. But now she knows that, with strategies and thoughtfulness, she can survive. An eightieth birthday party is in her memory-bank now too, and she hopes – and believes – it will be of benefit to her in the future.

Philip's struggle was going back to work after his wife's death. He had a senior management position in a major bank with national responsibilities. His employers had been extremely supportive and very sensitive after the sudden onset of his wife's illness and her untimely death. Philip was forty-one when his wife died. Sensibly, he took some time off work afterwards and, with the help of HR, made good use of the space he had. There was no pressure to go back to work – no 'should' in Thelma's terms – but he needed to return, to find a structure and a renewed purpose for his future.

'It was the right thing to do,' he told me, 'and gave me so much of what I needed. But it was still a struggle going home. Turning my key in the lock was, at times, very hard indeed.' Perhaps the return to work was a mistake after all, Philip thought. But he stuck with it. 'It was likely to be the way of things,' he told me, 'moving from one world to another with all the stresses that contained – and each time going home to an empty house.'

I spoke with him one day about how things were unfolding for him. The tears were getting less, he told me, and he felt he was coping better. Work was stressful but enjoyable. Promotion was in the wind. Life was looking and feeling good. 'And I've changed the nameplate on my door,' he said. He was about to move on to something else when I stopped him.

'That sounds like a big decision,' I said.

'No,' Philip replied. 'I just changed the nameplate.'

'But that's significant,' I suggested.

'No,' he insisted. 'It was just wrong, so it needed to be changed. It said: "Mr & Mrs" and that's not the case any more. So I went down the hardware shop on Saturday and got a new one with just my name on it. No big deal. Just making it right.'

Philip has passed that nameplate hundreds of times since his wife died and since he'd gone back to work. Whether he'd never noticed it before or seen it and decided to do nothing about it is neither here nor there. But he'd changed something that needed to be changed when he was able to do so. A big deal for me, though no big deal for him. But, for both of us, a real sign of hope.

Johnny, Thelma and Philip, in their losses and decision-making, are neither special nor different. They are what you are. They are where you are. And as they are and where they are, in small ways or in big ways, they offer us the reassurance that hope is always possible.

In *Nicholas Nickleby*, Charles Dickens has a friend offer this advice to the young Nicholas:

*'Hope to the last!' said Newman, clapping him on the back.
'Always hope; that's a dear boy. Never leave off hoping; it don't*

answer. Do you mind me, Nick? it don't answer. Don't leave a stone unturned. It's always something, to know you've done the most you could. But, don't leave off hoping, or it's of no use doing anything. Hope, hope, to the last!'

'Don't leave off hoping,' says Newman. That's exactly what Johnny, Thelma and Philip would say to you too – and so, certainly, would I.

Spring

Barren earth, it's all we see around us –
Hills and fields;
Lanes and paths;
Still and cold.
It's winter, after all.

Frozen earth, when icy weather comes –
Hardened ground;
Dangerous;
Rutted too,
When winter does its worst.

Muddy earth, churned by wind and rain –
Sticky glaur;
Dirty shoes;
Wellies' time,
As winter has its way.

Broken earth … spring's rousing times –
Longer days;
Gentle touch;
Warm embrace,
When winter fades away.

Stirring earth, awakening again –
Bleary-eyed;
Stretching out;
'Face the day',
The calling-card of spring.

Fertile earth, now hidden seeds burst forth –
Fragile shoots;
Shades of green;
Hopeful signs;
It's springtime, after all.

Living earth, your cycle comes around –
Death to life;
Pain to balm;
Brown to green;
New hope for summer days.

13. *See* https://archive.org/details/webereaved00hele/page/n3 *and* https://www.goodreads.com/book/show/37401715-we-bereaved
14. *See* https://www.guideposts.org/inspiration/inspiring-stories/stories-of-hope

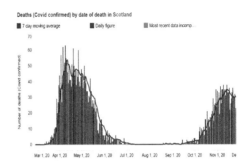

Deaths (Covid confirmed) by date of death in Scotland

■ 7 day moving average   ■ Daily figure   ■ Most recent data incomp...

Chapter 14

Bereavement and Covid-19

Built on a lifetime of engagement with bereaved people and their issues, the bulk of this book was completed in 2019. For as far back as I can remember, bereavement issues have followed relatively predictable patterns. Notwithstanding recent changes in societal norms, developments in funeral rituals and evolution of grief theory, human nature is as it always was. Grief is grief. Loss is loss. People grieve as they should. Reactions to loss are as they always were.

Our task therefore, now and always, has been to understand these normal patterns of loss, react to them appropriately, build around them necessary and helpful structures of support, and create an environment of healing and restoration for the good of individuals in their bereavements and to the benefit of all of society. So this book arose out of an understanding of the relative predictability of how we respond to loss.

Then, in March of 2020, we were hit with the global pandemic of Covid-19.

At one level, such a major, life-threatening issue should make little difference to the aspects of loss which this book seeks to tackle. People die and people are bereaved, and of course a pandemic will increase the risk of these deaths. With more than 140,000 deaths in our own country directly related to Covid-19, there are many people who are bereaved because of the spread of this awful virus.

But, if grief is grief, even though there are more people than normal who will be grieving for the loss of a loved one, they will still have to process their loss in a predictable, human fashion. If loss is loss, we will simply have to adjust to dealing with more people seeking to cope with loss than in past times. Within that, the individual response to loss is unlikely to change.

But not so! The effects of the Covid-19 pandemic cannot be dismissed as 'simply more of the same'. More than a year into this disturbing period of our lives, our society is already far from being the same as it was, and individuals within it are no longer the same as they used to be. The psychological, emotional, physical and spiritual responses to loss in a pandemic crisis are likely to profoundly alter the way people grieve.

A colleague reports that a young person currently being supported in their bereavement journey said, 'I'm relieved that [my loved one] died last year instead of this year as the restrictions would have changed my whole grief experience. I feel blessed to have been able to experience my grief in a "normal" way.' I suspect this voices the feelings of many people. But sadly, for those who have experienced loss during this pandemic, what might have been considered 'normal' before is no longer so. Research is telling us that there are some disturbing factors to be considered.

Let's go back to basics. Grief is the response we experience when something or someone we love and care about is taken away from us. It is fundamental to the human condition. It affects how we function in all aspects of life, and is therefore multidimensional. It can be anticipated by some, and be unexpected for others, and both of these will raise their own issues. But there is a commonality in all types of death, and indeed in all kinds of loss. In addition, grief is experienced across all ages and cultures and, as we've explored earlier, is not given the 'preparatory focus' or the energy and thought we put into other aspects of our lives. As a result most of us, most of the time, are unprepared for death. When we experience grief, therefore, and it affects us mentally, emotionally, physically, socially and spiritually, we don't have the necessary tools to hand to deal with what's happening to us. It's as if we've been catapulted into an alien world we neither recognise nor wish to explore.

Thus far, we might consider all of this to be 'normal', and, as I've suggested earlier, this is the framework in which I, and all those seeking to support people in their bereavements, have operated for a long time. Grief *is* a normal reaction to loss. And we know – from our own experience, from being aware of those around us and from the insights of professionals – that we will gradually move towards an acceptance of loss which, though extremely difficult at times, will bring us to some kind of understanding of a life that can be lived well and healthily. We manage the basic activities of life until we find glimpses of pleasure and fullness. We live as best we can until we know once more what real living can be.

There are predictable patterns to grief too, as we know, and though the grief journey will throw up its own idiosyncrasies depending on the bereaved individual, for many if not most of the bereaved there are no residual or serious social, psychological or life-limiting consequences.

Covid-19 changes that, and there are a number of grief factors which are highlighted and indeed exacerbated because we are living in a pandemic.

Among them is a process called 'anticipatory grief'. Will my loved one get this virus? If they have it, how bad will it be? If they go into hospital, will they get worse? If they end up in ICU, is that a step towards the end? If they're on a ventilator, are they likely to die? Anticipatory grief was something I lived with for fifteen years as a hospice chaplain. We expect that in a hospice. But we don't expect it to be around us as a matter of course in our families, communities and hospitals and constantly on the news.

Then there is the rapid onset and progression of the disease. From infection to death can be a matter of weeks or days. And this was particularly prevalent and shocking in the early stage of the pandemic. Like many others, I was scared of what I saw and heard about Covid-19.

We know, of course, that illness and any end-of-life timeline can be unpredictable. When my aunt was diagnosed with cancer, she and my uncle were told that she should 'expect to have six months or so'. She died within four months. My uncle, in his distress, was angry that the doctor had 'stolen two months of her life'. He hadn't, of course, but my uncle, like many, many others, was not prepared for the unpredictability of those final months, especially when death comes more suddenly than had been anticipated.

I have a colleague whose father died three and a half weeks after a diagnosis for prostate cancer. So we know it's an issue. But when it becomes *more* of an issue, and a much more *common* issue than before, we are ill-prepared for its implications. How do we cope with decision-making? How do we share with a loved one in their final hours when we can't even sit with them? How do we get our head around the speed of death? How do we not feel cheated when a love one dies quickly and someone else survives?

Alongside this, there is the trauma of a death. It's well documented that traumatic deaths, and the images they leave with the bereaved, can cause major issues in the grief journey. You can imagine, for example, discovering someone after a suicide, or witnessing a stabbing, or being a passenger in a fatal car crash. But such traumas are not limited to dramatic events. I worked with a woman who had been phoned at work to be told her father had had a stroke. By the time she got home, her father was being stretchered into a waiting ambulance. It was the last image she had of her loved one, and she struggled to move on from that.

I supported a man for several years who had the same issue after the loss of his wife. She'd been in the garden, and he called her in for a cup of tea but got no response. So he went outside and found her collapsed on the lawn. He gave her CPR while calling 999 at the same time. He continued with CPR till the paramedics arrived, but to no avail. He was consumed by his sense of failure to bring his wife back to life.

So take yourself into an ICU ward at the height of the pandemic – machines; medics and nurses in PPE; tubes; screens; respirators – that's if you were permitted to be there at all. Or maybe you're just impacted by what's shown on TV. And how do you cope if you're phoned to be told your maiden aunt had been moved from her nursing home into hospital and died the same day? However you experience a death in a pandemic, the trauma can have a major effect.

In addition, there's what is called 'disenfranchised grief', simply the sorrow of missing final moments, or not being able to grieve or prepare for a death as you expected to. This might be because of the suddenness of the death or the awful experience of not being permitted to sit with a loved one when they are dying. It doesn't take much to work out the devastating effects 'unfinished business' can have on loss.

Feelings of guilt, failure, anger and even blame can be contributory factors too. Again, we know these deep feelings are common in grief. But exacerbated they can be difficult to deal with. And there's plenty of research which tells us that when people don't have 'norms' to work with, when they feel lost and uncertain, when they experience helplessness, when they have to deal with 'disempowerment', their grief journey can be severely destabilised.

Finally, there's an issue which I can relate to well enough, even though I've not experienced personal losses in this pandemic directly related to Covid-19 ... How do we avoid the reality of death when it's around us all the time? This is 'collective grief': the day-in-day-out focus on death and dying; endless statistics of infection rates, hospital admissions, daily deaths; images of overflowing critical-care wards; news from all corners of the world of more deaths; daily press conferences by politicians, virologists and other assorted medical and psychological experts. We can't get away from death, it seems, such that on the one hand it feels overwhelming, while on the other hand it can make your own loss seem small in comparison – both of which make our bereavements worse.

There's a great deal of good research around complicated grief or complex reactions to loss. While most grief reactions fall within the patterns of 'normal' – and the majority of this book offers reassurance to those who are struggling with loss and wonder if their bereavement issues are normal or not – there are some whose reactions to loss are 'complicated'. Complicated grief has been medically categorised as 'Persistent Complex Bereavement Disorder'. When grief is a recurrent, persistent, painful emotion; when there is intense longing or yearning for the deceased; when unresolved symptoms such as bitterness, numbness, hopelessness and feelings that life isn't worth living don't dissipate or respond to immediate support; when grief is unnaturally prolonged ... we are in the area of 'complicated'. Numbers affected? No one is very sure, although one study by Lundorff *et al* in 2017 indicates that between 10 and 20% of bereaved people exhibit signs of complex or complicated grief. There is still much to investigate and learn about all the factors at play, but we do know that there are many risk indicators.

Before a death, these are pre-existing trauma; other losses; unstable relationships; pre-existing mood disorders.

Around the time of a death, these include dealing with a loved one who is chronically ill; the change of role of a carer; unfinished issues; the trauma of the death; lack of support.

After a death, we have to take seriously aspects of social circumstances which can destabilise a person and threaten their ability to deal with loss. These include isolation; limited resources available for support; inadequate physical contact; loss of control of arrangements; inability to fulfil the wishes of the deceased; family conflict. All of these can interfere with the natural mourning process.

It's not rocket science, therefore, to see that some or indeed all of these 'risk indicators' may be exacerbated by what we have to live with through this pandemic. A study on acute grief in the Covid-19 pandemic (due to be published in January 2021) suggests 'Higher grief levels occur among people bereaved due to Covid-19 compared to people bereaved due to natural loss. We predict that pandemic-related increases in pathological grief will become a worldwide public health concern.'

Simply put, bereaved people are likely to be more vulnerable now than they were when I set out to write this book more than a year ago.

It's worth noting also that research indicates that children who were isolated or quarantined during past pandemic diseases were more likely to develop acute stress disorder, adjustment disorder and grief. Thirty per cent of the children who were isolated or quarantined met the clinical criteria for post-traumatic stress disorder.

We might also ponder a final Covid-related issue … One phenomenon that has emerged out of this pandemic is what we now call 'long Covid', showing that people can carry the ill-effects of coronavirus for a long time after the original infection and traumatic period of illness. Likewise, we have also to be aware of the effects of 'long bereavement'. This is not something new, for in one way or another we all have to live with 'long bereavement', because the effects of loss will never leave us. But it may be exacerbated by what's been happening to bereaved people in recent times. For most of us, thankfully, the bereavement process will be no different from what it might have been in normal circumstances. But for some the effects will be deeper and longer-lasting and harder to bear.

In the face of this, there is much to think about, but to my mind four things become most important as we deal with bereavement during these unprecedented times.

Firstly, we – and I include myself in this – have to recognise that while the majority of people will still grieve 'normally', even in a global pandemic, a minority (an ever-increasing minority according to current research) of bereaved people will need specialist interventions and/or mental health support. And if these complex needs aren't obvious or measurable, an opportunity to assess what these needs might be is an important first step. Indeed, assessment, and dispensing with what might be easy assumptions, becomes all the more important. We need to begin with a clear indication of what level of support is needed.

Secondly, when the need for such support is identified, it has to be actioned quickly. And herein is a major problem. In the same way that we've had to increase frontline services during the pandemic to ensure that the 'acute' services in hospitals and ICUs are not overwhelmed, might the same not be true as we seek to respond to the increased needs of those who are bereaved? But if there wasn't sufficient bereavement support available *before* this pandemic, what is available now is likely to be even thinner on the ground or severely overstretched currently and into the future. My own involvement with the Stepping Stones and Acorns bereavement support services has seen their programmes – predicated on group-work, physical closeness and human interaction

– having to be discontinued, and there is no clarity as yet about what will replace them.

Thirdly, all of us should have a heightened awareness of the needs of those around us. At one of her recent daily press conferences, I heard Nicola Sturgeon, the First Minister of Scotland, say something I'd never heard a politician say before: 'Be kind to one another,' she suggested. 'Be loving. Be aware. We're all in this together. Offer a smile. Take care of each other.'

We're all in this together is an interesting description of where we are. Of course, we're all dealing with the same issues, but we react in different ways, even within the same family unit, for example. Someone said recently: 'We're in the same big storm, but we're in different boats.' So we have to be respectful of each other, and recognise the different ways people will grieve. We know that losses can have a severe and specific effect on individuals. A colleague told me recently of an elderly gentleman who'd been shielding for a long time during the lockdown in the first half of 2020, who in a session one day disagreed with the phrase about being in it together, saying: 'I've lost a whole chunk of time in the final years of my life, while there are many people who have decades ahead of them. I've lost what they haven't lost. I've lost so much more.'

There is no right or wrong in this, and there's no competition! This pandemic affects us all. There are individual and specific losses within it, but we're all victims of what's happening. So, from that individual perspective, an increased awareness of the effect of this pandemic on all who are bereaved should be a given. Information, support, human awareness *from* all of us *to* all of us is what's needed.

And in that sense the First Minister is quite correct. Let's care for people's immediate needs, even more than we've always done. Comfort and consolation can still be offered even though human

contact isn't available to us. Electronic communication has a lot
to commend it! We can offer support with practical tasks too, and
do all we can to promote resilience, self-worth and coping strategies. And, of course, helping people connect and reconnect with
social support is vital – even within the restrictions on us all.

Above all, we have to remember the approach with which I
began this chapter. Grief is grief. Notwithstanding all the additional factors in play at the present time, bereaved people will still
react the way they should. There may well be an increase in the
numbers of those who exhibit signs of complicated grief. But those
who do will still be in the minority. Even though grief may be wor-
sened by the Covid-19 crisis, the majority of people still need our
reassurance of the normality of their response to their loss. The
window of tolerance to loss remains very wide.

Let me close by sharing two personal stories about dealing with
death during this pandemic.

The first is about the death of my friend Andrew. My wife and
I had known Andrew since he was a small boy, and had seen him
grow into a highly respected adult. We followed his career as a
teacher in primary school, saw him fall in love and get married,
delighted in the development of his skills as a church organist.
Andrew died at the age of 48, leaving behind a grieving mother,
Betty, his husband Brian, and many, many good friends, including
both of us.

Brian and Betty invited me to help them plan, and then conduct,
Andrew's funeral. Because of the Covid-19 restrictions, numbers
at the crematorium were limited to 20. There could be no singing,
no crowds standing at the back, no physical contact, and everyone
had to wear masks. In 'normal' times the crematorium chapel
would have been packed. The singing would have been uplifting.
There would have been hugs and kisses. And almost certainly
everyone would have been invited to a large shindig afterwards in

Andrew's memory. But all of that was not to be.

We co-created the funeral service. Brian, Betty and I prepared a thoughtful and appropriate event for Andrew. We included opportunities to listen to recordings of Andrew playing the organ. Two friends offered appropriate readings. I read a tribute Brian and Betty had prepared, and included my own thoughts and contributions throughout the service. The funeral lasted 25 minutes. We didn't linger at the end.

The service was 'live-streamed' via the crematorium's system. Some of Andrew's teaching colleagues were outside in the crematorium grounds watching the service on their mobile phones. Many others – family, friends, colleagues, church folk – were following the service at home, or in school, or at work, all over the city, throughout the UK and, indeed, all over the world.

The service worked for those who were grieving the most, a mother and a husband, and for the few other folk who were privileged to be at the crematorium. It was intimate, gentle, 'appropriate to the occasion', as someone remarked. A friend suggested to me recently that the most important quality of any culture is its ability to adapt. Adaptation was fundamental to the preparation and delivery of Andrew's service. A lengthier service, with more elements to it and more people participating, such as would have been possible or even expected several months ago, wasn't workable now. But this much-simplified event felt real, effective and personal, and worked appropriately for me

At the same time, many more people had been able to participate – and genuinely to feel involved, according to feedback – in the service 'online'. No travelling was needed. No 'missing out' if you couldn't get there. No time off work. No stress.

Some might feel that the utilisation of webcasts for funerals is unnecessarily voyeuristic, creating a feeling of intrusion on other people's grief and not truly experiencing it as you usually might expect in person. While I understand this, it appears that this is not borne out in practice. This process of adaptation and a willingness to find and work with a new balance of intimacy and wider engagement, necessitated by the Covid-19 restrictions, has begun to show signs of being effective and helpful.

This has been reflected by many people with whom I have spoken during this pandemic. We *are* finding new ways – perhaps more honest and effective ways – to prepare and plan funerals. Gone are the 'productions', the performance, the overwhelming nature of funerals, to be replaced by the simple, the intimate, more thoughtful events. Does this make for 'lesser' funerals? I don't think so at all. Indeed, it may have the lasting effect of pulling us back from the 'pretence' of the 'big occasion', and may even be a better starting point for the realities and honesties of loss than has been the case in recent times. We're having to learn and benefit from the principles of adaptation.

Looking beyond immediate family and familiar paradigms to embrace new norms was never going to be easy. But, as we are faced with the reality and necessity of doing so, good things are emerging

The second personal story centres on the death of another friend. I won't name him, for his death is still raw and painful for me. He had been a colleague in my professional life, and we had supported each other through times of personal difficulty and tragedy. Retired and widowed, he lived a long way away. We communicated by text – his mobile phone contained his whole life, he once told me – and we met up for a beer three or four times a year when he was visiting Edinburgh or when I went to see him. The depth of our friendship was never threatened by distance or time. We always picked up where we'd left off last time.

In October 2020, I texted him to ask how he was, and since our opportunities to share a beer together were likely to be 'off the agenda' for some time yet, perhaps we could have a FaceTime or Zoom catch-up soon. I got no reply. A few days later, my wife and I did a bit of research and found his death notice in the press. He'd died suddenly four months before.

'Funeral private because of Covid-19 restrictions' the newspaper notice said. No word of a contact person. No invitation to participate online. No opportunity for people 'out there' who were grieving to get together – even virtually – to mark his death. Indeed, in different circumstances, I may even have been invited to conduct the funeral service myself, given the conversations I'd had with my friend on a number of occasions. But none of that was to be.

I'm not angry. But I remember how disappointed I felt. This pandemic had deprived me of joining with others and bidding farewell to a unique individual. To be honest, as I write this, I'm still processing my grief and the shock of finding out about my friend's death in such a disturbing way.

I've recently managed to make contact with some of the family, and that has helped a lot. We've talked about the circumstances of the death, and about how hard they also found processing things because of the restrictions placed on them. One day, we've agreed, we'll meet up and do what we've not been able to do up till now. Hopefully, that will offer some closure to us all.

In the meantime, I'll be thinking about my own ritual ... I'll put together my own way of saying goodbye. I think a couple of beers and a glass or two of single malt might be in there somewhere. And so will tears, and laughter, and poignancy, and reminiscences. But, apart from my wife, I have no one with whom to share any of that, and I'll miss out on a big chunk of my journey of grief.

The challenge of the Covid-19 pandemic, therefore, is to recognise that the beginning of our bereavement journey has to be fundamentally altered. For better or for worse, we have to do things differently. Get them right, and everyone benefits. Get them wrong, and complications and complexities may result.

There is much talk about living with a 'new normal' when all of this is over. At one level, any new normal will be the same as the old normal. Grief is grief. We will grieve as we must and find ways through the pain of loss. We have to. We have no choice. And we will do it and do it well.

But, at the same time, we must recognise that things will have changed, in the short and long term. Because of Covid-19, life – individually and collectively – will never be the same again. We have to find and build on new ways that will work as a supportive structure for those who are bereaved.

The 'new normal' may, in some respects, be healthier than the old one if, simply put, it allows us to be more focused on death and dying than we have allowed ourselves to be for a long, long time.

Differently

'We'll have to do it differently,' he said.
'I know that,' I replied. 'Everything's different now.
We can't do what we used to do –
have a big gathering ... sing her favourite hymns ...
kiss aunt Matilda ... It's the regulations.
We can't do what we want to do.'

'But what about the Wake?' he said.
'No chance,' I replied. 'Everything's different now.
We can't do what we always did –
go down to the *Rose and Crown* ... no stories and laughs ...
no round of drinks ... It's the regulations.
We can't do what we can't do.'

'But we'll have to do something,' he said.
'I know that,' I replied. 'But everything's different now.
What can we do that'll be OK?
What other folk have done? The funeral director might know …
perhaps we could ask … There are regulations.
What can we do that'll work for us?'

'We could break out the whisky,' he said.
'You're right,' I replied. 'She knew it would be different now.
Didn't she joke about the whisky?
"Give them a miniature as they leave … raise a glass …
there's your toast … Bugger the regulations.
Do that for me, OK?"'

'We'll do it differently,' he said.
'You're on!' I replied. 'For her sake, it can be different now.
Twenty miniatures, no problem.
Any single malt will do … the off licence is open …
we'll hand them out at the Crem … It's not in the regulations.
But it'll be important for us all.'

'We did it differently,' he said.
'We did indeed,' I replied. 'It was very different now.
We couldn't do what we used to do –
But we all had our whisky … and toasted her memory …
and I kissed Aunt Matilda … That's in her regulations!
You have to do what you have to do.'

Chapter 15

Beyond the ramparts

When my grandsons were small, I took them to Tantallon Castle, a semi-ruined mid-14th-century fortress, a few miles east of North Berwick in East Lothian. It sits grandly on the edge of a cliff, over-looking the Firth of Forth. It was, so the signage informed us, the last medieval curtain-wall castle to be constructed in Scotland. But my grandsons weren't bothered about signage, or history, or construction issues. They just loved old castles, and as we ex-plored the dungeons and great hall, the courtyard and turrets of Tantallon Castle, they were back in medieval times, fighting battles, waving swords and conquering invaders.

The best part for them (though a bit of a struggle for me) was being high up on the battlements, moving along the tops of the ancient walls, and being – as one of the boys shouted out for all to hear – 'the king of the castle'. And as we stood and surveyed the panorama around us – with the castle protected on two sides by the cliffs and the sea, and a clear view on the other two sides for miles around of any marauding hordes who might threaten to attack – it was easy to figure why Tantallon had been built where it was, and why people would feel secure and protected while they were safe within its sturdy walls.

I have had the same feeling as I've stood on the walls that were built to protect cities and towns from attack. When you see the purpose and strength of the protective walls around places as diverse at Lucca in Tuscany, Tallinn in Estonia and Londonderry in Northern Ireland, or even fragments of such walls in Carlisle, York or St Andrews among other towns and cities in the UK, you can see why such protective fortifications matter. They offer safety to those inside.

It is this image of protective walls and the space outside them that offers the beginning of a reflection for this final chapter. For while I have focused throughout this book on images, stories and ideas relating to aspects of loss with which bereaved people can identify and from which, I hope, they can draw some solace and insight, I want before I conclude to turn my attention to those who care for bereaved people and how they might better understand and fulfil their important role.

In a recent bereavement group, I was both moved and encouraged by a question from one of the participants. Belinda was trying to pick up the pieces after the death of her sister. She was clearly taking on board, and benefiting from, the insights shared among the team, resource staff and participants as the weeks went by. But towards the end of the penultimate session she asked, 'So what have we learned about our own bereavements that can assist us to help other people in the future who might turn to us for support and encouragement?'

It was a moving moment, and a powerful testimony to how someone, in the midst of their pain, can be aware of the needs and distress of others. But it was also an encouraging moment, for it articulated a question for all of us, programme team and participants alike: 'What *can* we do to help those who are bereaved, and how can we do it well?'

I hope the issues covered in the preceding chapters will have offered some clues to the nature of the lives being lived after a death, so that those of us who are called to care will react with more understanding and sensitivity towards those who are bereaved. There is no 'chapter and verse' about what to do in every situation. There is no 'answer 32B' to 'question 32B', no filing cabinet of pre-written responses, no rule book to memorise so we will always get things right. We will do what we are able to do. And unless we're completely crass and insensitive, anything we do will be helpful. We will make mistakes, of course, but if we offer our humanity, with all our flaws and brokenness, we will meet people in their pain so that healing can begin.

I want to emphasise, therefore, that doing what we need to do and doing it well begins *not* with a series of 'dos and don'ts', but with getting our attitude right. I used to say to students on placement with me when I was a parish minister that at funerals people seldom remember the details of what you say, but they will always remember the attitude you adopted and the atmosphere you created. In working with people who are bereaved we might do well to heed similar advice. And that's where we turn to the image of the strong walls of our castle.

It's not an exact science and, of course, like any metaphor it will creak and break if it's pushed too far, but I want us to consider that those of us who care – and in this case, those who are not themselves currently struggling with bereavement – are, in some fashion at least, in a place of security and strength. In that sense, we live in a secure castle, a place which is as familiar as it is safe, as protective as it is sheltering. There may be scary places outside, but we are assured that the castle walls will stand firm against anything which might pose a threat to our peace and security.

We are reminded, of course, in those times when we walk around the castle ramparts and see what lies beyond, that there are places of danger beyond our walls. And we can be pleased and relieved that we are not 'out there', at the mercy of the unknown and all the fears that we know exist in those places which lack safety and protectiveness. In bereavement terms, we are content that it's *others* having to live with such things and not those of us inside our castle.

So, imagine this … One day when we are walking our ramparts, we hear a cry from the distance. As the mists clear, we discern that the shout is coming from a traveller outside our castle. This is no dangerous army or marauding horde threatening us. This is simply a traveller who is lost and alone, and who is crying out for help. We see distress and we hear the cries. We see exhaustion and we hear pleas for assistance. We see someone unable to journey any further and we hear heartfelt entreaties for support. So what are we to do?

We have choices, of course, for that is what safety and security give us. We have time to make up our mind. But we may be frightened, still fearful of what is outside the walls, afraid of abandoning our security. Yet the lost traveller is still lost and still distressed, and we know, with all our human compassion, that we have to do *something*.

So we take the easy option. We stay on our ramparts and we shout back. We offer our advice and guidance. We give directions and instructions. We beckon the traveller to come towards us, because we believe they will be safe where we are, where we feel they should be. But we never move. We're too fearful to do anything that might pose a risk to our own safety. Yet our shouts may be lost in the wind or be too faint to make a difference. And even if the traveller hears them, they may make no sense, for they still feel alone. The lost traveller knows nothing of us that will allay their fears and nothing of the castle we inhabit. So our shouts make little sense. We feel that *we* have done what we can, and we're satisfied with that. It's the traveller's problem if they haven't done what we've asked them to do. Job done? No!

OK, so that's not enough. Another option, therefore, would be to take the risk, open the castle gates just a little, rush out towards the traveller, grab them by the arm and drag them, with all urgency, back to our castle so that they too can be secure. We are now safe again, and so we believe the traveller to be too. But is this the castle in which they wish to stay? Was this the way they were heading before they got lost? Did we ask about their hopes and fears, or did we just assume – because of our own fear – that we know best where the traveller should be? Mmmm …

Another option? Yes, there is. We could do what bereaved people need us to do, yearn for us to do, and that is to meet them in their lostness and wait with them till they have a clearer understanding of where the next stage of their journey will take them. So we have to be where they are, and be fully engaged with their fears and distress. And we must wait with patience, stilling our own anxieties, laying aside our own certainties and securities, taking the risk of being afraid ourselves … and all because that is what the weary traveller, the lost soul, desperately needs.

It is not enough to stay on our castle walls and shout advice. It is not effective for us to drag people into our framework of certainty and security without a 'by-your-leave'. What is needed is for us to go beyond the ramparts, into the scary, unknown world where the traveller is lost, and fully 'be' with them in our common humanity, knowing and believing that this is the beginning of healing and wholeness, purpose and hope.

On one of the most stressful days in the hospice in my time as chaplain, I'd had a series of particularly difficult circumstances to deal with and was pretty much at the end of my caring capacity. I wanted to get home so I could have some 'me' time and be ready for the following day. I was leaving the building when one of the nurses stopped me and said, 'Before you go, would you mind popping into Room 7 to see Sadie's family. She's not got long, and I kind of promised them you'd look in before you went home.' To be honest, I could have hit her. But I didn't. Well, you don't, do you? So I said, 'OK!' with a distinct weariness in my voice.

I knew Sadie well, and I'd spent time with her earlier in the day. She was widowed and had no children, but I knew that she had two sisters who were regular visitors, though I'd not met either of them before. So, having deposited my coat and briefcase in the nursing office, I headed for Room 7. The door was ajar, and I saw Sadie in her bed. There were two other women in the room, one sitting by the bed holding Sadie's hand, the other standing by the window with her back to me. 'Hello, I'm Tom, the chaplain,' I said. The woman by the bed nodded but said nothing. The woman by the window didn't turn round and remained silent. I assumed these were the two sisters, though neither of them made any attempt to introduce themselves to me. They obviously had nothing to say, and I didn't know what to say either. So, taking my cue from them, I stood for a while in silence.

The depth of quietness in the room was broken only by the unevenness of Sadie's breathing, the occasional sniffle from the woman by the bed, and me stretching for a box of tissues. I have no idea how long I was there. It was probably no more than a few minutes, but it seemed like an eternity. Eventually, I took my leave. 'I'm just going to slip away now,' I said quietly. 'Thank you,' said the woman holding Sadie's hand. The woman by the window said nothing. My sense of inadequacy when I left the room was quite overwhelming. It was a bad end to a bad day.

When I got to work the following morning, Room 7 was empty. Sadie, I learned, had died during the night. To be honest, I was relieved. Mid-morning, one of the nurses came to my office to tell me that Sadie's sisters were back to collect her belongings and the necessary paperwork and were asking to see me. So, a few moments later, I was being introduced – properly this time – to Jacqui and Barbara, Sadie's younger and older sisters, though I was seeing Barbara's face for the first time. They were upset, but, once they'd pulled themselves together, Jacqui said they had a couple of questions about funeral arrangements and the like. We took ten minutes or so to deal with some simple issues, enough for them to be reassured and for me to feel that at least I'd been able to offer something constructive. I rose to take my leave, shook Barbara by the hand, and was taken aback when Jacqui gave me a spontaneous – and lengthy – hug, sobbing on my shoulder as she did so. Eventually, regaining her composure, she said, 'Thank you so much for all you've done.' 'Not at all,' I replied. 'I'm just happy I was able to help today.' 'Oh, not just today,' she continued, 'even though this has been very helpful. Babs and I were just telling the nurse here how helpful you were yesterday, coming in to see Sadie, and us. You were just terrific, you know, just terrific.'

I was stunned. And after I'd mumbled some words of appreciation, I left them in the nurse's care, went back to my office and tried to work out what had just happened. Going to see them in Sadie's room had been enough. Remembering my reluctance and tiredness of the previous evening and recalling my sense of uselessness and the overwhelming nature of my silent inadequacy, I was glad that going to see them had achieved much more than I could ever have expected.

Broken people, lost travellers in a scary world, had been met in their lostness, and even my silent presence had been enough to reassure two grieving sisters that all was not lost. And Jacqui's hug – and Barbara's handshake too – were just the teaching and affirmation a weary hospice chaplain needed. They were important 'whispers of wisdom' for me.

I hope that in this book some more of those 'whispers of wisdom' have found a louder voice. I hope that the stories of bereaved people I have worked with will help you understand the normal processes of grief and will offer some insights into how you might cope with them.

The majority of the people whose circumstances I have shared throughout this book have been anonymised. Genders, relationships, ages and dates have been altered to allow their story to be told. And where that isn't the case – such as the account of Andrew's death in Chapter 13 – I have permission to tell their story. But the voices of all of them are real and honest. The whispers are theirs and not mine.

There are three words that come up all the time in the final review sessions of our bereavement programmes: the first is 'privilege', for it is indeed a privilege to be invited into the world of loss people inhabit and to journey with them through their sorrow and joys; the second is 'trust', for it is only when a non-judgemental trust has been established that people feel safe enough to open up with each other and explore real and important issues; and the third is 'confidence', for to see people, even over a short number of weeks, grow in confidence in their own understanding and resilience makes it all worthwhile.

One woman put it this way. 'You know my husband was a plumber,' she reminded us, 'and so he never went anywhere without his bag of tools. I never knew what was in his bag. That was his world. But *he* knew what was there, because he had everything he needed when he needed it. So what I take away from this programme is a new tool-bag for my bereavement. I know some of the things that are in it, and I know I can reach for them when I need them. Thank you all for that. But I also know there are a lot more tools in this bag that I've not used yet. I don't know what they're for. I just know they'll be there when I need them, when there's a job I have to do that I haven't done before. So I'll take away a tool-bag, because I have the confidence to believe that everything I need will be there when I need it. And I know you'll all have your own tool-bag too.'

That's why it's a privilege to do the work I do. And that's why I value such 'whispers of wisdom' – for that is surely what they are – that I can communicate, softly or loudly, through these pages, to anyone who needs or wants to listen.

Walls

Big walls you build to show the world your strength;
Barriers; daunting, exclusive
To those on the outside,
Or the other side
Of your great walls.

Ramparts – permanent, safe, secure,
Well built; rising high; signs of strength
For those on the inside,
Or on the right side
Of your proud towers.

Iron gates – keeping the stranger at bay;
Locked up; barred against intruders.
'No entry here; please keep out.'
The signs shout it loud.
'You're not welcome.'

Sentry posts – guardians of the righteousness
Of the few against the many;
The privilege of birth;
Accident of class;
The 'them' and 'us'.

If you would build your walls to keep you safe,
Might there be a place for me inside?
Can I be included,
Join you on your side,
Safe together?

If you would raise your turrets big and bold,
Might I see them from a distance
So I can know safety
Waits for me inside
Your ramparts strong?

If iron, fettered gates you must construct,
Let them yield to the cries of one
Who's lost and fearful now,
And needs the welcome
Of an open door.

Call down your sentries from their watching posts;
Bid them now to offer what I need –
Rest for my weary bones;
Peace for troubled thoughts;
Love for my soul.

Postscript

When grief
is easier to hold

What insights do we hope to leave with people after they have engaged for a time with any bereavement support structure they might be offered? That, I suspect, will be for them to tell you, for different people will take away different things that they will know are appropriate to their journey of loss. Insights, coping strategies, ideas, clarity, boosts to confidence, calmness, perspective and much more will be specific to individuals and to their own experiences of loss.

There is, however, one aspect of loss which is common to everyone, and one which we seek to emphasise throughout and particularly at the conclusion of our bereavement programmes. It is simply this: the grief which is crippling at the beginning of a loss will, in time, become easier to hold.

In our final session, after we have shared what we've learned and the confidence we've taken from the process, and before we take our leave of each other (another kind of loss for people to cope with) I place on the table a small wooden bowl filled with pebbles. These stones, I explain, have been gathered from beaches, shores of lochs and riverbanks from throughout the UK. They have been collected from wherever I travel, and in their shape, colour and size exhibit the well-known variety of such pebbles. They are all misshapen but rounded, their sharp edges having been smoothed off, ground down, by the effects of river-flow and tides, stone on stone, stone on sand, over thousands of years.

What were once sharp shards of rock, chipped off a great cliff, are now the rounded pebbles with which we are all familiar.

If we were to have picked up one of these stones when it was sharp and jagged and held it tightly in our hand, it would be painful to hold, because its spiky edges would cut into our skin, its rough corners would cause us damage. But if we take one of these pebbles now, or pick one up from a shore or a riverbank, we can close our fingers over it, feel its smoothness to our touch, and hold it tightly in our hand with no pain at all.

This is what happens when we hold our grief. At the start, as we hold it tightly (and it is ours to hold, for not only is the shape and colour of our grief unique to us, but no one else is going to hold it for us) it is painful; it hurts; it cuts us. And the tighter we hold it, the harder and more painful it is to grip. But over time this grief becomes easier to hold. The sharp edges are smoothed off. Although it cuts us painfully at the start, over time – perhaps a long time – it isn't so acute. We still have to hold it (for no one has taken it from us, nor will they). It is still unique and distinctive in its shape and colour, and it will be ours to keep for ever. It is still different from everyone else's grief. It is our personal loss. But over time … it has become easier to hold.

So people are invited to take a pebble from the bowl … to remind them of the promise – the heartfelt promise – that while their grief is still to be carried, and that it remains personal and unique, it becomes easier to hold as time goes on. They are encouraged to carry their pebble with them, to keep it in their purse, or handbag, or trouser pocket, and to take it out, and hold it, and feel it, and examine it, to bring back to mind the promise that has been given to them in our bereavement support work. But holding that pebble will also remind them of the group with whom they've shared an important part of their life, a little part of their bereavement journey.

Some people in our groups continue to meet up after a bereavement programme has ended. And I know – because they tell me – that they talk about the time they've shared together and what's happening to them now. Many of the people I've worked with in the past ten years still have their pebble – and I know, because they tell me … and they know too, for themselves, that the promise we gave them was true.

Grief becomes easier to hold over time. That's a whisper of wisdom that a small, rounded pebble in your hand can offer to you too.

Comments on another book by Tom Gordon:

New Journeys Now Begin
Learning on the path of grief and loss
ISBN 9781905010080

The moment you pick up Tom Gordon's book and start to read it you realise that this book has been written by someone who knows what he is talking about. It is a book written from the heart, a book that is grounded, gritty and honest, a wonderful resource for those embarking on the painful journey of grief and loss.

This book is for real. It doesn't talk around the deep issues of life and death; it takes us right into them. It has within its pages stories which are deeply emotional, but it also has a lightness of touch and real humour. This is a book that l would have no hesitation in recommending.

From *Coracle* reviews

This book is not prescriptive but contains many useful insights for both the bereaved and those helping the bereaved on their journey of grief. It is written sensitively and in a most approachable manner. Well worth reading.

Church of Scotland minister (Amazon review)

Having recently lost my much-loved husband to cancer, this book has been so helpful and I found that I could identify with so much that Tom Gordon has written. He manages to cover even the smallest of everyday experiences that affect you so much when bereaved. He has a very deep understanding of people and the way in which loss and grief affects your every waking moment. The poems are amazing and beautiful, even though they make you cry. They certainly reflect exactly how you feel at various stages on this horrendous journey of grief.

I would recommend this book to anyone suffering loss and grief and I am sure it would be a great resource for any organisation or any counsellors working in this field.

How Tom knew exactly what I was living with, I shall never know. Weekends … anger … loneliness … unfinished issues … they're all there, and they're all mine. Thank God someone out there actually understands.

Bereaved relatives